DEMOCRACY

DEMOCRACY

Jack Lively
St. Peter's College, Oxford

BASIL BLACKWELL · OXFORD

ISBN 0 631 15460 4

Set in Intertype Baskerville
Printed in Great Britain
by Western Printing Services Ltd, Bristol
and bound at the Pitman Press Ltd, Bath

Contents

One

INTRODUCTION

The objective of this essay is to define democracy, or at least to trace some of the boundaries of its meanings, and to assess the strengths and weaknesses of different modes of theorizing about democracy. Such an enterprise may seem beyond reasonable ambition, it may even seem positively dangerous, since the term has become so soiled by use that its employment on any delicate conceptual surgery carries grave risks. For the word has a thriving life in the world of practice as well as in the world of theory. Over generations men have struggled to create it, wars have been fought in its name, it is brought up in justification of many different political systems and of quite opposite policies. The Russians and the Chinese join with the Americans and the British in describing their polities as democracies; the Labour Party aims at social democracy, whilst the Conservative Party has set its sights on a property-owning democracy. In face of this welter of proprietary claims, one understandable reaction has been to dismiss the possibility of the concept being used in serious political discourse. It is not, on this view, a sensible tool of analysis or even a coherent ideal, merely a 'hurrah' word, a propagandist device indicating approval of whatever is the practice or policy or institution to which it is applied.

There is, however, no compelling reason for accepting such determined Pyrrhonism, no compulsion on us to allow bad usages to drive out good. Indeed, the very fact that the term is so persistently and so ardently canvassed in the ordinary language of politics creates a need for it to be given as great a coherence and clarity as is possible. Yet the sceptical response does underline one reason for the ambiguities surrounding the concept. Democracy is certainly a 'hurrah' word in the sense that, in the contemporary world, there are few who will take an explicit stand against the legitimacy of democracy. Since the discrediting of fascist doctrines in the Second World War, we are apparently all, or nearly all, democrats. It was not always so. In the early nineteenth century, even a Nonconformist could publicly declare himself against. 'Wesleyanism is as much opposed to Democracy as it is to Sin', said Jabez Bunting, president of the Methodist Conference.[1] And throughout the nineteenth century there was no dearth of critics of democracy. By 1949, in contrast, nearly all shades of political opinion were agreed on its desirability.[2]

Given the well-nigh universal acceptance of the legitimacy of democracy, few regimes are now willing to declare themselves avowedly undemocratic and most wish to present their democratic credentials. On self-description, Rhodesia, South Africa and Tanzania as well as Russia and America are democracies; even military regimes commonly seek justification by pledging themselves to the ultimate restoration of democracy (usually in that purified form resulting from the elimination of politicians). There is no need to take all these claims at face value. There may be good grounds for denying that a regime can make itself a democracy simply by calling itself one. The term can cover a variety of institutions with no more than a family resemblance between them, but this does not mean it is infinitely flexible and can be used without any discrimination. Nevertheless, the almost universal approval given to the word and the very general desire to appropriate its prestige makes the task of elucidation more difficult. It also means that any attempt to define democracy (or the perhaps easier task of what is not democracy) must involve some commitment to political positions, some positive evaluation of the justifications proffered for different kinds of political system.

[1] Quoted in G. M. Young, *Victorian England: Portrait of an Age* (2nd ed., Oxford, 1953), p. 66.
[2] See the UNESCO survey *Democracy in a World of Tensions* (Paris, 1951), p. 527.

Another source of ambiguity is that the word now operates on two levels, in the world of reality as well as in the world of ideals. When Jabez Bunting declared his opposition, it was clear that he was countering an ideal, a system which did not exist although many radicals were by then urging it. Now, however, the word is used to describe actual systems whilst still retaining its ideal connotations. There *are* liberal democracies and peoples' democracies. Problems arise in consequence, not just because entirely different systems are brought under the same term, but also because it is unclear how we are to elucidate the concept. If we ask what are the purposes of democracy, or how a democracy works, or even what a democracy is, it is not clear what materials, what procedures, we should use in seeking answers. Should we still be trying to define in the abstract the purposes of democracy and suggesting the institutions necessary to the serving of those purposes? Or should we be looking at democracies as they exist to provide answers?

There can be little doubt that the second strategy has been the more extensively pursued since the last war. The orthodox view has become that definition of the ends served by democracy or of the institutions appropriate to it must be built up from empirical inquiry into Western democratic systems.[3] At the same time, and as a consequence, democratic theory has less and less attempted its traditional task of providing a critique and radical evaluation of existing polities. Only very recently has this task been reasserted as a proper end for political thinking.

A good deal of this book will be concerned with assessing the merits of these two strategies. Here, we can look briefly at the reasons for the present hegemony of the second. Perhaps one of the most important reasons for the retreat of political theory from its role of recommendation has been its monopolization by academics. At one time, political theory was a concern of many educated men, and particularly of practising politicians themselves. Now, with the increasing division of intellectual as of other labour, it has become largely professionalized and confined to universities. There may be good sociological reasons why academics

[3] The term 'Western democracy' will be used throughout the book to denote existing representative systems of the Anglo-American type.

as a group are inclined to timidity or at any rate a dislike of open commitment to political positions. More specifically, there have been two academic trends in recent years which, in their application to the study of politics, have prompted a retreat from recommendation.

The first has been the aspiration to render the study of society scientific. Any such enterprise of course involves a host of initial analytic difficulties which have not often been resolved or even faced in the confused empiricism commonly brought up in defence of political science. It is, however, usually accepted as one entailment of this commitment to scientific inquiry that the investigator must eschew any value positions, or at any rate must regard any personal political concerns as an extra-curricular activity. How do things work? In the present context, how do democracies work? Answering such questions is the proper employment of a truly scientific scholar. How should things be? What must we do to improve democracy? To attempt such questions is improperly to import ideology into scholarship.

Developments in philosophy have also favoured the retreat. At least in Britain and America the dominant schools since the war have been positivistic and linguistic. The first, with its insistence that sure knowledge is possible only on an empirical base, has at once given support to the scientific aspiration and foreclosed discussion of political objectives as an area where only personal preferences are at issue. Linguistic analysis has defined the philosophic tasks largely as the disentangling of the purposes and structure of different kinds of inquiry and the clarification of the concepts utilized by them. This too has led to a general disavowal of any philosophic obligation to argue for substantive moral or social values. The extreme edge of advocacy has seemed often to be the promotion of a little gentle mental hygiene, the therapy of clear thinking.

These intellectual trends go a long way towards explaining the comparative quiescence of recent political theory and the absence from the ranks of the theorists of men like those of an earlier generation who saw theory as an essential precondition of social and political reconstruction. However, they do not entirely explain the change in attitudes towards democracy. There has also been a lapse of confidence in the democratic ideal, a pessimism about the possibility or even the desirability of extending its compass, either by the creation of new democracies or by the further democratization of the old. These fears and doubts have taken shape in a number of debates, amongst which those on bureaucracy, elites and mass participation are the most significant. Of necessity, we shall have to return to these subjects more than once, but it is worth noticing initially that the common thrust of arguments in these areas has been towards a deflation of democratic pretensions.

Since Weber, it has become common to characterize the modern age in terms of a bureaucratic organization, whose operational principles are rational efficiency, hierarchy and neutrality. This organizational form, it is claimed, transcends function, being common to all sorts of organization, both governmental and non-governmental, and it transcends ideology, being common both to the capitalist and communist worlds. Again, since Weber, it has been usual to picture this development as an inevitable outcome of industrialization. Modern technology leads to the increasing division and specialization of labour, and in turn to the growth in complexity and size of organizations. The larger the scale of organization and the more technically demanding its functions, the greater is the need for clear articulation of an organizational hierarchy, precise delimitation of the tasks and power of each level, clearly established lines of responsibility upwards; in a word, the greater is the need for bureaucratic organization. There is in consequence a supposed tension between the needs of modern industrial society and democratic ambitions. For the import of the argument is that democratic control over those performing management functions, be they in the state or the non-state sector, is certainly difficult and perhaps also irrational. The difficulty and the irrationality arise from the same fact, that democratic control implies the subjection of the expert to the ignorant. The problem is not of course a purely theoretical one. There are very real and pressing questions concerning the relation between elected and bureaucratic bodies and the protection of the citizen against administrative abuses. Nevertheless, the way in which the problem has been posed theoretically does present a gloomy prospect from any democratic viewpoint. If there is a choice at all, it seems to be a choice of either the affluence created by industrial society and its attendant bureaucratic structures or whatever benefits further democracy might bring.

Elite theories have carried the pessimism even further, for the burden of their message is not just that non-democratic forms of organization will characterize modern society, but that a democratic form is itself an impossibility. All organizations, no matter what their formal structure, will be dominated by small elites. Even those most openly dedicated to democratic principles are subject to what Michels called the 'iron law of oligarchy', under which the leadership of organizations is bound to escape any forms of real control from below. As we shall see, something like these assumptions have been carried over into a good deal of recent democratic theory. The dominance of elite groups is accepted, but the possibility of a specifically 'democratic' system is nevertheless maintained, the peculiar and characteristic feature of democracies being, not the absence of elites, but the presence of an open competition between them. Something then is salvaged from the wreckage, but many older democratic hopes are lost. And elitist arguments at least encourage the view that it would be foolishly unrealistic to mourn them for long.

Perhaps the severest shock to democratic confidence has been a decline of faith in the common man as a receptacle of liberal virtues. Historically, democratic movements have been spurred by two basic beliefs—in the innate virtue or rationality or common sense or capacity for judgement of ordinary people and in their immanent potentiality for resenting and resisting oppression. Twentieth-century history has shaken the adherence of many to these articles of faith. Modern dictatorships have sought their legitimacy in popular support and, in both their fascist and communist forms, have gone to considerable lengths not to stifle but to stimulate political interest and popular participation, at least of a symbolic kind, in political affairs. Moreover, totalitarian and illiberal movements—the Nazi movement in Germany, the Fascist movement in Italy, the Peronista movement in Argentine —have in fact enjoyed very considerable popular support. Probably the most traumatic and influential experience, however, has been that of American academics during the McCarthy era. The extent of popular backing for McCarthy's peculiar brand of illiberalism and demagogy, much of it directed against the professoriate, not unnaturally helped to turn American political science away from at least the more innocent hopes of the American populist tradition. Such suspicions have been confirmed and intensified by studies showing the latent authoritarianism widespread in lower-class groups and the frailty of their hold on democratic norms. The dilemma apparently posed is that further democratization, further involvement of the masses in politics, might well prove fatal to liberal democracy.

The situation surrounding discussion of democracy is then confusing. Well-nigh universal approval combines with considerable disagreement about the objects of approval; there is much uncertainty about the theoretical frame in which the discussion should be set; and there are many doubts about the validity or practicability of pressing the democratic ideal to anything approaching its limits. These ambiguities should determine the structure of the inquiry. We must attempt to give some meaning to the '*rule* of *the people*' and to trace at any rate roughly the kinds of institution or practice which can be said to embody it. We must look at the types of theory that have been utilized in analysis of democracy. Finally, we must distinguish the various ends which might possibly be realized or maximized in a democratic system.

Two

THE MEANING OF DEMOCRACY

At first sight, there seems little difficulty in defining democracy. The term has a long history and has been applied with some consistency to a form of government in which the 'demos', the people, rule; in which political power is held by the many rather than by the one or the few. In other words, it has been used, in conjunction with terms such as monarchy and aristocracy, to describe a particular distribution of power within the community. Traditionally, the trilogy has been employed to distinguish situations of monopoly, of oligopoly and of equality. This identification of democracy with political equality has prompted an extended use of the term, democratic, covering any application of the principle of equality.

Despite the apparent absence of difficulty, merely to state the simple definition is to run immediately into a host of definitional ambiguities. If democracy is the rule of the people, what constitutes 'rule' and what 'the people'? Does talk of 'the people' imply some homogeneous will amongst all members of a given community, capable of expression in universally agreed political decisions? But, if a democracy requires such perfect harmony of views, is it possible? Can we ever expect, would we ever want, a society in which political differences were permanently stilled? This kind of doubt is reinforced by the fact that the concept of popular sovereignty has historically been used by regimes to justify suppression of opposition which (it has been said) is hostile to the will of the people as defined by the rulers themselves. In face of such apparent perversions of the notion, one natural reaction has been to identify democracy with the majority principle. Not the people but the majority is sovereign. It will be one of the objects of this chapter to examine the majority principle and to see how far it can be maintained as a defining principle of democracy.

The other obvious ambiguity in the notion of the rule of the people lies in the word, rule. There are difficulties on two sides here. On the one side, it could be said that in any strict sense the many cannot rule, while on the other that in any loose sense the many may rule, and usually will, in any political system. If to rule includes the right, the authority, to command others, a democratic system no less than any other will require some concentration of rule in the hands of a small number. If popular rule is taken less strictly to mean that the majority decides on the broad lines of government policy and legislation, it can and has been argued that this is empirically impossible, since in any organization, whether or not the majority has the formal right to decide, the actual decisions will be taken by small groups of leaders; and the larger and more complex the organization, the more pronounced will be this trend. However, if by popular rule we mean only that the government will take into account and broadly follow the wishes of the many, widely differing types of regime would be said to be systems of popular rule. Any practical handbook for governors would have, as one of its first injunctions, the advice to follow the wishes of the masses, other things being equal. Given these ambiguities, it will be the second object of this chapter to examine what meaning or meanings can be attached to the term 'rule' when we speak of popular rule.

1. THE MAJORITY PRINCIPLE

Lord Bryce defined democracy as 'government in which the will of the majority of qualified citizens rules'.[1] This formula associates democracy closely with the majority principle, but it also leaves somewhat uncertain the application of the principle. For there

[1] *Modern Democracies* (1921), vol. I, p. 26.

may be two questions at issue when we speak of democracy as the rule of the majority. The first is the question, 'Who is to make the decisions in a community?' Who, in Bryce's phrase, are to be the qualified citizens? The second is, 'How are those who make the decisions to reach them?' If the majority principle is the defining principle of democracy, then presumably, for a system to be democratic, firstly the decision-makers must comprise a majority of the community and secondly the procedure to be followed by the decision-makers must be that the preferences of a majority of them decide. It will be argued that neither of these assumptions is wholly tenable and that the majority principle is not invariably compatible with political equality.

The extent of citizenship

Let us define a citizen as one who takes part in political decision-making. The first question then amounts to this; is a democracy a system in which the body of citizens comprises a majority of the members of a community? That such a system would have a strong claim to be called democratic might seem obvious. But consider the case of a community the majority of whose members are under the age of eighteen. Would we wish to say that the restriction of citizenship to those over eighteen rules out the system as a democracy? Consider too what might seem to be alternative cases in which women or blacks are in a small minority and are denied citizenship. Would we wish to say that, despite the restriction of citizenship to males or whites, the system is democratic since the majority are citizens? It would clearly be hazardous to assert that the democratic answer to each of these questions must be yes; yet this is what would be implied by defining citizenship in terms of the majority principle. There do seem to be circumstances in which, in a democracy, a majority may be excluded from political life and other circumstances in which the exclusion of minorities would be undemocratic.

We can conclude that the 'many' in the rule of the many need not necessarily be a numerical majority of the community. Is there any principle which can link together in common justification the exclusion of a majority (those under eighteen) and the non-exclusion of small minorities (women or blacks)? Appeal might be made to some notion of political competence. In the first example, it could be said, all those who are politically competent are being treated as political equals and only those who, on account of immaturity, cannot be supposed to have the qualities necessary to citizenship are excluded. In the second case, the exclusion of blacks or women denies citizenship to some who are as politically competent as those to whom citizenship is granted, whites or males.

Obviously enough, it is not sufficient to say that the defining principle of a democracy is that all who are politically competent should share equally in citizenship. For the boundaries of competence might be drawn so narrowly that the citizenry is a very small class indeed. Indeed, it might be said that the difference between political systems along this dimension of the location and distribution of power is not that a democracy is concerned with citizenship whilst other systems are not, but that its definition of who is competent to be citizens is wider. The extent of citizenship will depend on what qualities are taken as necessary to political competence and what the distribution of those qualities in the community is, or is taken to be.

What attributes are regarded as necessary to competence will be related to what are accepted as the ends or purposes of the political system. If, for example, the point of the system is taken to be the security of property, it makes sense to argue for the restriction of citizenship to those with a 'stake in the country'. On the other hand, starting from the claim that governments should attend to all wants and interests or that a regime should allow wide opportunities for the political education necessary to self-development, the relevant qualities are the possession of wants or interests, or the ability to express them rationally, or the capacity to engage in public activity.

Whilst the definition of competence will depend on the posited purposes of the system, the boundaries of citizenship will be defined also by the distribution of what are taken to be the relevant qualities. The democratic case has consequently included both a statement of the proper purposes of the state and also an assertion that the appropriate aptitudes are possessed by well-nigh all in the community. Whether the relevant capacity is to

B

express coherent wants, to calculate interests, to make rational moral and political judgements, or to assume an active public role, the case has typically proclaimed it as a universal attribute. Or, at the least, the main thrust of modern (as distinct from Greek) democratic thought has been to demand that all be treated as capable of citizenship unless very strong evidence of personal incapacity is produced. At the same time, it has typically rejected exclusions on grounds of social characteristics. So infancy and insanity have been accepted generally as good reasons for exclusion but not poverty or race.

This does not of course dispel all ambiguity. Those who wish to exclude from citizenship on grounds of, say, race might argue that all members of the group at issue are personally incapable in some crucial respect—perhaps they are all culturally backward or less than normally intelligent. The democratic response might start from questioning whether cultural backwardness or less than normal intelligence constitutes evidence of unfitness for citizenship. Even granting these are sufficient grounds for exclusion, the democratic argument would then hold that race nevertheless is not itself the relevant criterion. All those who are culturally backward or of low intelligence, regardless of race, should be excluded and decisions would necessarily have to be based on an examination of individual cases.

Clearly there is still considerable room for argument. At what age should the vote be granted? Should criminal conviction lead to a loss of civic rights? Should there be a literacy requirement? Such questions will no doubt persist. What is obvious is that they cannot be resolved by reference to the majority principle. Except by implication, the democratic case has not been that the majority of a given community should rule but that citizenship should be granted to all the politically competent and that competence should be assumed unless there are strong grounds in individual cases for exclusion.

Majority decision

The majority principle cannot therefore be seen as the basis for determining the boundaries of citizenship. Is it any more convincing to say that the principle of majority decision is a procedural principle peculiar to democracy? Is it a uniquely democratic answer to the question, 'How are those who take decisions to reach them?', that the preferences of the majority must decide? Clearly this is not so. The problem of how decisions are to be reached is not one that arises only in a democracy. Nor is it only in a democracy that the principle of majority decision might be thought appropriate. The problem will arise in any decision-making group. A group of hereditary nobles might wish to adopt a procedure by which they as a group can come peaceably to a decision. And they might find the procedure of majority decision the most appropriate. So the procedural principle of majority decision is not in any way unique to a democracy.

However, it might be claimed that, although not unique to democracies, majority decision-making is peculiarly appropriate to them in that it, more than any other procedure, ensures equality amongst decision-makers. To test this proposition, let us look schematically at the ways in which a group of any sort, be it a democratic electorate, a representative assembly or a committee, might come to decisions and then assess how far these different procedures ensure equality to its members. In practice, the number of possible procedures is almost infinite, but some main types can be listed.

Firstly there might be a *unanimity requirement*. The procedure would be that no policy could be adopted unless all voters were agreed upon it. It is important to notice that, put another way, this procedure would grant to each individual the power to veto decisions, or at least to veto fresh initiatives, for any single individual could by abstention or opposition, foreclose a particular proposed option.

Secondly, there might be a *stipulated majority requirement*. The procedure would be that a stated majority must be reached before any policy could be adopted. There are many possible variations on this procedure. The stipulated majority could run from an absolute majority (over 50 per cent of the vote) where more than two alternatives are posed, or a majority of eligible voters where only two alternatives are posed, to something just short of unanimity. Put another way, this procedure amounts to the granting to minorities of a veto over decisions, the precise size of the minority capable of exercising the veto being determined by the terms of the stipulation.

Thirdly there could presumably be a *minority requirement*, which would stipulate that the alternative with the smallest number of votes would win.

Fourthly, there could be a requirement under which decisions would be made by *interested minorities*. In this case particular minorities would hold the power of deciding in particular areas, different minorities deciding in different areas. Clearly in one sense, the question of how the decision is to be made is simply transferred, for the question of what procedures the minority group itself is to use in order to reach a decision remains open.

Lastly, the procedure could be *simple majority decision*, that is that whichever alternative gains the largest number of votes wins.

One general point should be made here, which is that none of these procedures will necessarily guarantee a decision being reached. In all of them, there may be circumstances in which the formula cannot be applied. This is perhaps most obviously the case with the unanimity or stipulated majority procedures. If two alternatives are being considered, both of which would alter the *status quo*, it could well be the case that unanimity or the stipulated majority might not be achieved for either.

However, it is also the case that under the simple majority procedure it might be impossible to reach a determinate decision or at least it might be impossible to reach a determinate decision compatible with the requirement that the preferences of the greatest number should prevail. The instance that springs to mind immediately is when an equal number of votes is cast on both sides of a question. In such cases, in practice, appeal has to be made to a different rule, such as weighted voting where the chairman is given a casting (additional) vote. There is a less obvious, although now much discussed, possibility that no majority decision can be reached where there are more than two alternatives and where the voters' orders of preference are taken into account. Say that there are three alternatives a, b and c and three equal groups, I, II and III. Group I prefers a to b, b to c, and a to c: Group II prefers b to c, c to a and b to a: Group III prefers c to a, a to b and c to b. In any straight vote amongst the three alternatives, an equal number of votes would be cast for each. If the alternatives are paired, then a two-thirds majority is achieved for each alternative. As between a and b, Group I and Group III prefer a to b, as between a and c, Group II and Group III prefer c to a, and as between b and c, Group I and Group II prefer b to c.[2]

These particular difficulties in reaching a decision can of course be eliminated if only two alternatives are presented. It might be argued that systems such as the British and American avoid this dilemma by presenting to the electorate the choice between two major parties. Clearly the existence of only two major parties is not a sufficient condition to ensure a determinate majority decision since in both American presidential elections and British parliamentary elections it is possible for a party to win even if it has fewer votes cast for it than an opposing party, and likely for a party to win on a plurality of votes cast. A more significant theoretical objection emerges if we look at the relation between preference for party and preference for policies advocated by parties. For even if we concede that a two-party system ensures a majority in the choice between parties, it does not ensure that majority decisions are made in preference between policies. Let us assume that voting for parties is related to policies pursued or advocated by parties.[3] Obviously a majority vote for a party does not imply a majority preference for all the policies of that party. Say a party puts forward policies a, b and c. A referendum might produce a majority against a and b, but the party can still win if a majority favours c and believes the issues at stake in this policy are more important than those at stake in policies a or b. Less obviously, a majority vote for a party does not necessarily entail a majority vote for *any* policy put forward by that party. Suppose that a minority X prefers a to not-a and believes the issues at stake in a to be more important than those at stake in b or c. Similarly a minority Y prefers b to not-b and sees b as all-important; and minority Z prefers c to not-c and sees c as all-important. Provided that minorities X, Y and Z are discrete

[2] See Kenneth Arrow, *Social Choice and Individual Values* (New York, 1951), p. 3; Robert A. Dahl, *A Preface to Democratic Theory* (Phoenix paperback ed., 1963), p. 42.

[3] See below, Chapter Three, section 3.

and do not overlap too much, the party advocating a, b and c could muster a majority even though a referendum on each separate issue would defeat each of these policies. So, even if a two-party system can avoid the possible difficulties that might arise from a situation where more than two alternatives are presented, it cannot ensure that the preferences of a majority in terms of policy are successful.

The problems that arise in reaching a resolute decision under the simple majority procedure are replicated under other procedures. One amongst many possible objections to a minority requirement could be that, given more than two alternatives, all alternatives might achieve a minority in the same way as all alternatives might achieve a majority. In the case of decisions by interested minorities, since the minority group would itself have to have a decision-making procedure, the objections raised to other procedures would apply likewise to this. The possibility that a determinate decision cannot be reached is therefore present under any of these procedures.

The question to which we must now return is how far these different systems satisfy the principle of political equality and in particular whether or not the majority decision requirement is peculiarly appropriate for a democracy, supposing a democracy to be concerned with the maximization of political equality. In one sense, and that a weak one, all the suggested procedures can be egalitarian—for all are compatible with the stipulation that each person should have only one vote and each person's vote should be accorded the same formal weight in any count as every other person's vote. Looked at in this way, the principle of political equality is relevant only to questions of who is to vote and not to questions of voting procedures, apart from the procedural rule that each is to count as one and no one as more than one.

In another sense, these different procedures may satisfy the demands of political equality to different degrees. If we go beyond formal equality and ask how far these procedures assure any actual equality in the ability to determine decisions, differences may emerge. It might be helpful here to distinguish between retrospective and prospective equality. Looking at a decision that has been made, it could be said that retrospective equality has been achieved if everyone equally determined that decision. Looking at a decision about to be made, it could be said that prospective equality is achieved if no persons or groups suffer peculiar disabilities which prevent them from determining that decision.

No one determines a decision who has voted against it. Under a majority decision system, the losing minority do not determine the decision, and, so far as that particular decision is concerned, the members of the minority did not retrospectively achieve equality with the constituent members of the majority. Clearly, it is only if unanimity, complete agreement on a decision, is reached that complete equality in the retrospective sense is achieved. For it is only if all have agreed that all can be said to have determined *that* decision. Only with a complete consensus can retrospective equality be won, and no procedure allowing for a decision other than by universal agreement can assure retrospective equality. It might seem therefore that the procedure that requires complete consensus, the unanimity procedure, is that which most decisively satisfies the claims of political equality. This is not, however, the case. It is one thing to claim that only unanimity would achieve complete retrospective equality, quite another to say that a unanimity requirement would do the same. For a unanimity procedure does not ensure that complete agreement is in fact reached, nor even does it ensure that, where agreement is incomplete, no decision is reached. We have seen that deadlock, inability to come to a decision, might result from a unanimity requirement; if two alternatives, both of which would alter the *status quo*, are being considered and full agreement on either is impossible, no decision can be reached. Clearly, this is rather an unusual form for a decision. More commonly, the situation would be for a proposal changing the *status quo* to be put and voters asked to declare for or against it. Suppose that all except one vote for such a proposal. Under the unanimity procedure, the proposal would be defeated, but it is not the case that no decision has been reached. The procedure does not ensure that all are agreed on those decisions actually reached, for maintenance of the *status quo* is no less a decision than changing it, and in this instance the decision conforms to the preference of a single person against the preferences of all others. Patently any procedure that allows for, even invites, decisions by a single dissentient cannot satisfy the demands of political equality. Precisely the same arguments can be put against a stipulated majority requirement, for if any minority can block a proposal approved by a majority, it is effectively making the decision.

The dilemma was one faced, although not resolved, by Rousseau. His object was to devise a political system that would eliminate all ordination and subordination between men. He believed this end could be attained if all men determined the social rules binding them. Only if there were complete agreement on all social rules could all be assured equally of complete freedom, defined at least in part as 'obedience to a law which we prescribe to ourselves'. The demand Rousseau is making is for full retrospective equality, and he sees clearly that this can be approached only as decisions approach unanimity. On the other hand, he explicitly rejects any unanimity procedure and declares that a majority vote should bind the rest. In order to satisfy his own requirement of full retrospective equality, he has to argue that a defeated minority does not really express a different preference than the winning majority but is merely mistaken in its view of what the common good requires. So the losing minority really wanted what was in fact decided. By the doubtful assertion that a consensual agreement need not manifest itself in voting behaviour, Rousseau manages to reconcile majority decision with retrospective equality.

The most strenuous and explicit recent attempt to defend the unanimity rule is that put forward by Buchanan and Tullock, the authors of *The Calculus of Consent*. Their basic argument may be sketched quite briefly. Given a situation in which there is agreement on the distribution of property and assuming that no costs are involved in reaching decisions, rational egoists would choose a unanimity procedure as the means of reaching collective decisions. Private bargaining between individuals always leaves those involved better off, since otherwise no bargain would be struck, but collective governmental decisions may leave some worse off than before, may in other words impose external costs. The external costs an individual might expect to suffer will decrease with an increase in the number of individuals whose agreement is required for a collective decision. Only when the

agreement of all is required will the individual be sure that no external costs will be imposed upon him; therefore he would choose
the unanimity rule.[4] Now it is clear that this whole argument rests
on the assumption of universal agreement on the distribution of
property. What is more, the authors imply this is a continuous
agreement on the *status quo*. For they assume that, since no
individual would have his position altered except with his consent, an initial agreement will necessarily lead to agreement on all
subsequent distributions. Because most political conflicts in the
real world arise precisely from attempts to change the distribution
of goods, the unreality of this assumption is obvious. Nevertheless
one conclusion derivable from the argument is applicable to the
real world. This is that those rational egoists who wish to preserve
the *status quo* (although not all rational egoists) will choose a
unanimity or stipulated majority procedure as the means of
decision-making.

This constitutes the second count against these types of procedure from the standpoint of equality. As has been seen, they
do not achieve retrospective equality. Nor do they guarantee
prospective equality, since not every individual or conceivable
minority is equally capable of affecting decisions by vetoing them.
In practice, the power of veto is a much more effective weapon
in the hands of those who wish to maintain the *status quo* than
in the hands of those who wish to change it. A veto power can
prevent a proposal being carried, it cannot carry it. And since
proposals normally intend some change in existing circumstances,
the weight of advantage lies with conservative rather than radical
minorities, or even with conservative minorities rather than
radical majorities. A proposal that things should stay as they are
would be unusual, and, even so, a veto of it would not instate an
alternative, in the same way as a veto of a 'radical' proposal
instates the stay-as-you-are alternative. It could be argued that a
radical group could try to bargain with its own power of veto,
threatening future vetoes to try to muster a sufficient support for

---

[4] James M. Buchanan and Gordon Tullock, *The Calculus of Consent*
(Ann Arbor, 1962), pp. 63–8, 85–96. When the authors take into account
the costs of decision-making (which will mount with the number of persons whose agreement is necessary to the decision), they modify the
unanimity rule into a stipulated majority rule.

some present alternative. This log-rolling argument supposes, however, the absence of a consistently conservative minority. A minority taking up a stand-pat stance on every issue or most issues could hardly be covered by the threat of future vetoes of radical proposals. At the very least then it can be confidently claimed that a minority veto power (or, what amounts to the same thing, a unanimity or stipulated majority procedure) normally militates against prospective equality by reinforcing conservative rather than radical groups. Since conservative groups tend to be those advantaged by the *status quo*, such procedures tend to bring in political inequality to buttress social privilege.

Another procedure involving minority decision is what has been called the system of decision by interested minorities, under which powers in particular areas are assigned to subgroups of the whole, in some sense more interested in the outcomes within those areas than in the whole. In a sense, this is the model for any assembly with a system of strong and independent committees. Of more interest here is the suggestion that this procedure is the operative principle of Western democracies. The suggestion has been put forward most forcefully by Robert Dahl. One of his major arguments is that Western democracies, what he prefers to call polyarchies, are characterized not by majority rule but by 'minorities rule'. What distinguishes democracy or polyarchy from dictatorship is not the distinction between majority and minority government: it is rather one 'between government by a minority and government by minorities'.[5]

Broadly, there are for Dahl two processes which give to interested minorities, rather than to majorities, the power to determine or affect specific governmental policies in polyarchies. The first is the electoral process. As we have seen, even in a two-party system, elections cannot ensure that the preferences of a majority in terms of policy are successful. Competing parties may try to muster a majority by adapting their policies to the wishes of intense minorities, that is those whose voting decision will depend on the parties' attitudes to one special set of issues. What the majority might wish in regard to a specific policy will influence party positions only when the majority feel strongly on an issue or, if the majority are apathetic on an issue, the minority are

[5] Robert A. Dahl, op. cit., p. 133.

apathetic also. In the situation (which is likely to be the common one) where the majority are relatively apathetic and the minority intense, a vote-winning strategy for parties will dictate deference to the wishes of the intense minority. The second process by which, it can be said, 'minorities rule' is assured in real-world polyarchies, is the activities of pressure groups, acting on governments, bureaucracies, legislatures, parties, or public opinion to try to advance their own goals through favourable government policies. Again, the argument runs, it can be assumed that this process gives power to affect policies not to all minorities in all areas but to intense minorities within those areas of particular interest and importance to them. For it is unlikely that a group will incur the cost of organization and activity unless the policies it wishes to affect are in some way crucial to it. Dahl's conclusions are that the problem of the tyranny of the majority, which so exercised early democratic theorists, is illusory, since majorities do not decide. At the same time, the problem of allowing for intensity of preferences (which could not be achieved by simple majority decision) is solved by a system of 'minorities rule', under which 'all the active and legitimate groups in the population can make themselves heard at some crucial stage in the process of decision'.[6] The implication is that polyarchies are mechanisms for squaring the economic circle by establishing an inter-personal comparison of utilities.

How far is this rule of decision by interested minorities, and in parallel polyarchic rule, compatible with political equality? Clearly, the defence that it is compatible rests on the claimed virtue of the rule that it takes into account intensity of preferences. Whilst at first sight it seems to militate against equality by allowing minorities to overrule majorities, it effectively restores it by allowing each individual to affect those decisions crucial to him, even if he is in a minority. It is evident that the case that intensities of preference are taken into account by minorities rule rests on the presupposition that engagement in political activity is a function of relative intensity. For (assuming that only overt political activity is going to affect governmental policy) it is only if intensity of feeling is expressed in activity, and greater intensity of feel-

---

[6] Ibid., p. 137. See also pp. 145, 150.

ing in greater activity, that intensity of preferences will influence
government actions in due proportions. This presumption is made
explicitly by Dahl.[7] But in practice it is a highly dubious empirical hypothesis. The very desire to engage in political activity
may be dependent upon an individual's or group's perception of
the relation between such action and the satisfaction of his or
their felt needs; and such perceptions, varying as they may do
with educational attainment or subcultural background, may not
be uniformly spread in a community. Further still, it is at least as
likely that political activity is a function of the ability to act as of
the desire to act. The ability to translate a desire to act, no matter
how 'intense', into activity is patently likely to be unevenly distributed in the community. Organizational skills, time, money,
easy access to agents of government, parties or the media—these
are all necessary to the construction of effective political action
and all are attributes which are relatively inaccessible to many.
Those groups with resources that can be mobilized for political
action—in general those groups advantaged by the *status quo*—
will be those favoured by the rule of decisions by interested
minorities, if intensity of feeling is measured in terms of propensity to engage in political activity.

Even leaving aside the inequality of organizational resources,
some groups may labour under special disadvantages in seeking
to organize. The capacity of any organization to attract members
will depend upon the inducements it can offer. These may be of
two sorts, a promise to pursue some collective good common to
members or the provision of private benefits to individual members. Assuming self-interest to be an important motive for action,
those organizations which can provide private benefits will be
stronger than those whose only attraction is the promotion of
collective goods. For the pursuit of any collective goal is in most
instances irrational to the rational egoist, since in most instances
his involvement will not ensure the success of the enterprise, nor
will his abstention ensure its failure. Not all organizations are
able to provide extensive private benefits, and therefore not all
groups with a collective interest are capable of sustaining an
organization to press this interest. The Automobile Association

[7] Ibid., p. 134.

does perform a pressure group function, but probably most drivers join it because it offers breakdown and tourist services. In contrast, it is difficult to see what personal incentives might spur a poor man to join an organization of the poor even if it promoted the collective interests of the poor.[8] This again throws doubt upon Dahl's implicit assumption that all groups with a common interest are equally capable of throwing up a pressure organization.

Another flaw in the defence of 'minorities rule' is that a group already organized to influence decision-making, either through mobilization of its electoral resources or through direct action upon decision-makers, will not necessarily restrict its activities to areas in which it feels intensely. In other words, once a group has incurred the costs of organization, it might be worth its while to use its organizational strength to press for policies which only marginally benefit its members. If minorities were always starting from scratch, it might be plausible to argue that they will only undertake costly political activity in order to affect decisions on which they feel strongly. In practice, such a *tabula rasa* does not exist. Groups, or some groups, are already organized; and, since the costs of utilizing existing organizational strength are likely to be much lower than the costs of creating that organization originally, the policies followed by existing groups are unlikely to be confined to areas in which the benefits they can gain are large. Again, there are reasons for doubting if engagement in political activity necessarily indicates greater intensity amongst the activists than amongst the non-activists.

Finally, this procedure might advantage already privileged groups, not only because those groups are likely to command the resources necessary to political activity, but because they may feel more 'intensely' on a wide range of issues than less privileged groups. Any government policy that redistributes some good in an egalitarian direction will in one sense at least affect the previously privileged minority more than the majority. What each member of the minority can lose by the policy is at least absolutely greater than what each member of the majority can gain. There is therefore at least a likelihood that a system of

[8] This argument is elaborated by Mancur Olson in *The Logic of Collective Choice* (Harvard, 1965), particularly in Chapter VI.

'minorities rule' will be used particularly by privileged groups to defend their privileges.

There may be other grounds on which 'minorities rule' can be defended. It might, for example, be conducive to political stability. It is doubtful if it can in most circumstances be defended on democratic grounds, that is by the argument that it is conducive to political equality. It could be so defended only if all intense minority views were effectively expressed. In practice, it might well enable already privileged minorities to guarantee their privileges and even to push government policies in directions only marginally beneficial to them.

We are left with two other types of procedure—minority decision and simple majority decision. Clearly, a minority decision procedure would be absurd. Again, the distinction between who is to decide and how they are to decide is important. It is not absurd (although it is not democratic) to urge that those who should decide should be a small minority of the community. It is absurd to say that whoever decides should decide by a minority decision procedure. Obviously, if voters understood the procedure, it would in practice be converted into majority decision since voters would vote for the alternative they least preferred. Given this simple and obvious stratagem, the least preferred alternatives could never win and the procedure could never be followed. The point of raising this fanciful case is merely to show that the procedures discussed up to now are the only ones which can in practice allow for effective decisions by minorities.

By default, it would seem, majority decision is most conducive to political equality. In most circumstances this will be the case; but we should notice that majority decision cannot ensure complete political equality and in some situations it might militate against it. A majority decision cannot achieve retrospective equality, since the minority clearly did not determine that decision. Such retrospective equality can be achieved only when a complete consensus on some alternative is present, and no procedural rule of any kind can ensure such a consensus. Those rules which do demand complete unanimity or large majorities are not ways of creating or encouraging consensus but, as we have seen, modes by which minorities can generally decide. Majority decision has at least the common-sense advantage from the standpoint of retrospective equality that more people favoured the winning alternative than any other presented. Procedures that allow for minority decision have two disadvantages from the standpoint of prospective equality. In the first place, of course, even if it cannot be forecast beforehand whether a particular voter will form part of the majority or the minority, his chances of falling within a minority are less than his chances of falling within the majority; and, if a minority can decide, his chances of determining the decision must be smaller than his chances of not determining it. In addition, it may well be the case that the minorities who decide or veto decisions in procedures which allow for this are discrete and not shifting minorities. As we have seen, they might well form minorities favoured by the *status quo* or who wish to preserve the *status quo*. Since such minorities are distinct and fixed the chances of some voters being members of a minority which both wishes and is able to decide will be less than those of other voters, and their prospective equality is diminished.

It might be argued that the advantages of a majority decision system from the standpoint of prospective equality are complementary to the disadvantages of a procedure allowing for minority decision. Clearly any single voter's chances of being in a majority are higher than of his being in a minority. Equally it might be claimed that prospective equality is enhanced because, whilst the deciding minority can perhaps be identified beforehand in a minority decision system, deciding majorities are not discrete and identifiable. This has been another response to the fears of early theorists such as Madison or Tocqueville that the majority principle might lead to the 'tyranny of the majority'. As we have seen, one recent reply has been a denial that majority decision is the operative principle of Western democracies. Another has been that there is not a distinct, homogeneous majority deciding all isues as a group but a series of shifting majorities which change with different issues or at different times. Precisely because majorities are amorphous and indiscrete, the operation of majority decision does not exclude any group from determining at least some decisions. So far as this is the case, prospective equality is assured since no individual or group is going to find itself in the minority on every issue. Unfortunately this is not necessarily the case, for if there is an identifiable minority and a majority which does vote together on most issues, the 'tyranny of the majority' might prove a reality. The situation most feared by the early theorists was the 'oppression' of the rich by the poor. These fears that an inevitably numerically small wealthy class could be tyrannized by the poor majority have generally proved unfounded, perhaps because the rich possess other means of influencing decisions than through the ballot-box. The problem of a 'permanent minority' and its oppression can arise, however, when the minority has no or few means of influencing decisions beyond the vote. There may be a real possibility in some societies that the poor (relatively speaking) might become a permanent minority. Two more concrete examples that spring to mind are blacks in the United States and Catholics in Northern Ireland. In relation to such groups, the phrase 'majority tyranny' does have meaning, since they are identifiable minorities with relatively few means of influencing governmental policies. We should be clear about what the problem is here. The real problem is not that the democratic principle, that is the majority principle, leads to the oppression of minorities, and in consequence democratic norms have to be violated in order to give security to minorities. The problem is rather that in such circumstances, the majority principle does not secure the operational principle of democracy, political equality. For any procedure which permanently excludes particular groups from any ability to determine or influence communal policies cannot be deemed democratic.

When such a problem of a permanently excluded minority arises, it is not likely that a wholly effective solution in purely constitutional terms can be found. It is difficult even to say what sort of procedures might help towards a solution. It might be that some guarantees could be given to minorities by leaving certain questions outside the competence of majority decisions, through for instance 'entrenched clauses'. The minority might be given over-representation by some system of weighted voting. When a minority is geographically concentrated, a 'federal' solution might be appropriate, that is the devolution of decision-making so that in the smaller areas the permanent minority becomes a majority. Or procedures such as stipulated majority rule might be used to provide some veto power and thus some protection to the minority, although a veto provides little comfort to a minority if the original situation it can help to preserve is itself unsatisfactory. In other words, despite what has been said about procedures allowing for minority decision, there may be occasions and situations in which such procedures will work towards political equality. Equally, there are some circumstances in which limits on majority decision may be set on democratic grounds.

The question of what sort of procedural rule is appropriate to democratic decision-making is not capable of easy or *a priori* answer. We might give two cheers to Bryce's definition, 'government in which the will of the majority of qualified citizens rules', but admit that in some circumstances the fear of 'majority tyranny' is real, the principle of political equality can be violated by majority decision and therefore some procedure giving powers of decision or veto to minorities might be appropriate from a democratic standpoint. Generally speaking, such limitations of majority rule will be needed where there exists a minority permanently excluded from political influence. Where, on the other hand, minority decision-making buttresses the influence of already favoured minorities, it is difficult to see how it can be justified on democratic grounds, although of course this is not to say that no defence at all can be constructed.

Political equality

The discussion of political equality up to now might seem excessively abstract. It has been concerned almost entirely with examining which constitutional rules are conducive to political equality. This preoccupation could be criticized on two grounds, firstly that political equality cannot be assured by constitutional provisions but depends on all sorts of social arrangements affecting the distribution of influence on government, and secondly that it presupposes that it is useful to talk of citizens in a large and complex modern state making communal decisions. Both of these objections are justified.

Universal suffrage and the adoption of appropriate decision-making rules are insufficient to reach even an approximation to political equality. How far it is achieved will depend also upon

C

the distribution of the wish and ability to use the rights of citizenship and upon the extent to which resources other than voting can be used to affect communal decisions. Whether or not an individual engages in political activity, from the minimal extent of voting to the most extensive commitment of time and energy, is not just a question of personal taste. It is too easy to say that, given the absence of legal bars to political involvement, equality of opportunity has been established, and no further problems arise in establishing political equality.[9] Such involvement varies with the attitudes held and the resources commanded by an individual. It will vary with his own sense of political efficacy, his apprehension of the extent to which he can alter decisions governing his life, his access to information and competence in assessing it, his ability and willingness to pay the costs in time and money of participation, his experience of social organization. It may be that these attitudes can be affected by the political system itself and that, as many democratic theorists have hoped, the ability to participate feeds on experience of it. At the same time, the attitudes that encourage political participation, as well as of course the material resources necessary to it, are unevenly distributed in Western democracies. Family background, work experience, educational attainment, income levels, social status—all these factors affect men's propensity to act politically. Political equality will therefore necessarily vary with the achievement of equality of resources or similarity of experience in other fields. Clearly too, if the possession of wealth or control over mass media can give direct influence over decision-makers, inequalities in these possessions can result in political inequalities.

The dependence of political equality on other sorts of equality should not mislead us. Although equality cannot be established merely by constitutional arrangements, it cannot be established without some constitutional frame in which the governed can influence governmental policies or personnel. Universal suffrage and the adoption of appropriate decision-making rules may not be sufficient conditions of democracy but they are certainly necessary ones. This is the obvious but crucial weakness in the claims of the 'people's democracies' to be democracies. On one side, the charge

[9] This seems to be the view of Giovanni Sartori. See his *Democratic Theory* (Praeger paperback ed., 1965), pp. 87–90.

is made that in Western democracies, despite the formal equality of the franchise, the real source of power, ownership of the means of production, is engrossed by a small class. On the other side stands the claim that this inequality having been eradicated in 'people's democracies' and the state having only one interest to serve, the interest of the people as a whole, true democracy has been established. However justified the charge against Western democracies, and it has some force, the positive claim does not follow. It is one thing to admit that within a formally democratic system political equality may be greater as other equalities are achieved, quite another to say that if those other equalities are present then political equality is necessarily established.

The other objection to our previous discussion of political equality is that it unrealistically presupposes a lack of differentiation and hierarchy quite impossible to achieve in a large and complex modern state. For, the argument might run, even if there were no social and economic differentiations to create inequalities in political influence, the need of modern states for a sophisticated machinery of government will of itself produce an uneven allocation of political functions and consequently the articulation of an hierarchy. Whatever the possibility of a people governing itself in a Greek city state, it is mere romantic Hellenism to suppose this a realizable ideal in modern industrial society, which requires specialization of function and centralization of control. The need for a bureaucratic organization of the machinery of government must inevitably compete with the ideal of political equality and, at the least, limit the operation of rule by the people. We shall return later to the gravamen of the argument, but before we can say that rule by the people is impossible, we must be clear what might be meant by rule.

2. THE RULE OF THE PEOPLE

Possible requirements of popular rule

No one meaning but a range of meanings has been attached to the phrase 'rule of the people'. What might be the requirements which need to be satisfied for popular rule to be established?

Running from the strongest to the weakest, the range might be:

1. That all should govern, in the sense that all should be involved in legislating, in deciding on general policy, in applying laws and in governmental administration.

2. That all should be personally involved in crucial decision-making, that is to say in deciding general laws and matters of general policy.

3. That rulers should be accountable to the ruled; they should, in other words, be obliged to justify their actions to the ruled and be removable by the ruled.

4. That rulers should be accountable to the representatives of the ruled.

5. That rulers should be chosen by the ruled.

6. That rulers should be chosen by the representatives of the ruled.

7. That rulers should act in the interests of the ruled.

It is clear that the term 'popular rule' has been used to cover a large number of different relationships between government and governed. Is the problem then to discover which is the 'correct' usage, which requirements are necessary for a system to be democratic? In a sense, the answer is yes, since some of the weaker requirements are insufficient to constitute the basis for a system that may be called democratic. In practice, however, the problem is often which meaning or requirement is to be followed in particular circumstances. For different types of rule are appropriate to different contexts. To take an obvious (but not always appreciated) example, the requirement that all should be involved in crucial decision-making might be appropriate only to small communities or organizations. Even in small associations, there are limits of time and space to the participation of men in communal affairs. They may be unable or unwilling to spend too much time on them; and there may be insuperable difficulties in organizing meaningful debate in too large an assembly. Obviously, these problems mount with the size of the association. For reasons of economy and efficiency, men might prefer to act under a different and more limited requirement, such as that representatives be involved in crucial decision-making or that rulers be accountable to the people.[10]

The question of which requirement is appropriate in particular situations is at the centre of many of our constitutional debates. To what extent and in what ways should White House actions be subject to Congressional scrutiny and control? In what circumstances would impeachment of a President be justified? Is the British Cabinet responsible to Parliament or to the electorate? What is the meaning and what are the limits of ministerial responsibility? What should be the role of parliamentary select committees? Should there be a referendum on crucial issues such as British entry to the Common Market, or a general election, or should Parliament alone decide? Questions such as these could all be rephrased in terms of which requirement, if any, should be applied in a particular context.

Whilst such debates can be posed as decisions on the appropriate democratic procedure, it is apparent that conformity to a democratic norm is not the only standard to be applied. Nor is it by any means clear that it is the only standard that should be applied. If it were, the problem would be much simplified. We could take the strongest requirement, that all should govern, and reject any alternative as inappropriate. The democratic ideal, however, lives in a populated world, a world of other values which may properly claim our attention and which may not be realized or protected by democratic procedures. Where conflicts arise, it may only be possible to modify the strongest requirements or we may even wish to abandon democratic requirements altogether. We have seen already that the size of an association may make the demands of the strongest requirement impossible to fulfil. This is only one instance among many others. If we are discussing the relationship of the executive to representative bodies or the question of workers' control in industry, we cannot be concerned solely with what would democratize the situation further. Inevitably other questions such as, 'Can the government come to clear decisions?' or 'How will workers' control affect the

[10] The point has been made by Robert Dahl in *After the Revolution?* (Yale, 1970), pp. 40–56, 67–71, 82–103, at what might seem unnecessary length if one forgets the confusions of many of the demands for participatory democracy.

productivity or pricing policy of an enterprise?' will arise; and we may wish to adopt a weaker democratic requirement (or even to abandon democracy) in the light of the alternative needs raised by such considerations. This is not to say that greater representative control of government would necessarily produce greater uncertainty or ambiguity in decision-making, nor that workers' control would necessarily produce greater consumer exploitation. It is merely to suggest that the reverse is not necessarily true, and therefore the question may arise of balancing greater democratization against other values like facility of government decision-making or consumer protection. And this balance may be achieved in particular instances by accepting a weaker rather than a stronger requirement.

Insufficient requirements

Any particular political system may satisfy a range of requirements, and there is no inconsistency in settling on different standards for different contexts. We might, for instance, ask for the satisfaction of a stronger requirement in local government, the government of small communities, than in central government. Are there any of these requirements which are either impossible to achieve or in isolation would not be sufficient to render the system democratic?

The first requirement, that all the people should govern, might seem impossible to satisfy. Even a small community in which all met in assembly to enact legislation could not involve all its citizens in administrative tasks. Even in Athenian democracy, it was only members of the Council of Five Hundred, chosen by lot, who played an administrative role. And was it not the arch-apostle of participatory democracy, Rousseau, who asserted baldly, 'It is against the natural order for the many to govern and the few to be governed'?[11] Yet, if we pose the requirement slightly differently, and ask how far a political system allows for the involvement of private citizens in the work of public administration, we can see that the requirement is not entirely without

[11] *The Social Contract*, Book III, Chapter IV, in *The Social Contract and Discourses* (Everyman ed., 1947), p. 55.

meaning or reality. It is not only possible for the requirement to
be met in particular contexts; it is actually met at present in certain areas. The jury system is an example. Whatever other justifications might be provided, one defence of the jury has been precisely that it gives larger numbers of citizens experience (albeit
limited) of the administration of justice.[12] In Britain, the Justices
of the Peace are a body of amateur magistrates. Elected representatives in British local government do have extensive administrative powers and responsibilities. A system can then provide, for
some at least, the experience of ruling and being ruled: and,
although the amateur administrator will no doubt face mounting
distrust, it would not be impossible to devise ways in which this
experience could be extended, if such an extension was thought
desirable.

Are any of these requirements insufficient, even if met, to
render a system democratic? It will be argued that the last three
requirements are. This runs counter to some recent discussions of
democracy, for it has been claimed on the one side that governments which act in the interests of the many are thereby democratic and on the other that democracies are no more than
systems allowing the people or their representatives to choose
their rulers.

The first claim forms the basis for the communist appropriation
of the word, democracy. The case for the defence has been put
recently by C. B. Macpherson.[13] Originally, democracy was associated with class government. It meant rule by or in the interests
of the poor and oppressed. In this sense, Marx was a thorough
democrat. For him, the capitalist state was inevitably an in-
strument by which the bourgeoisie maintained its exploitation of
the masses and consequently its habitual dehumanization of men,
its distortion and impoverishment of human capacities. The
proletarian state, the rule of the many, would equally be a class
regime pursuing the interests of the many; but, the aim of this
class being to destroy capitalist ownership and its inhibitions on
human development, proletarian rule would transform the very

[12] See Alexis de Tocqueville, 'De la démocratie en Amérique' in
Oeuvres complètes (ed. J. P. Mayer, Paris, 1951–), vol. i (i), pp. 282–8.
[13] *The Real World of Democracy* (Oxford, 1966, paperback ed.), pp.
12–22.

nature of political relations. Twentieth-century revolutionaries, such as Lenin, have faced a problem Marx did not fully appreciate the inability of a majority whose attitudes have been warped by a debased society to realize in thought or in deed their full human potential. They have therefore been forced into acceptance of revolution and rule by a vanguard, able to discern, as the masses cannot, what needs to be done to regenerate mankind. Regimes established by revolutionary vanguards are not, concedes Macpherson, democracies in a narrow political sense, although there is every reason to suppose that they will develop into democracies of a one-party type. In a wider sense, they can very properly claim to be democratic since their final aim is human equality and, if they remain true to their purpose, they rule in the interests of the many.

There are a number of difficulties in this argument. Even apart from the historical judgement that Soviet regimes are actually developing towards intra-party democracy, there is the theoretical question of whether or not one-party democracy is logically possible. The argument must also embrace the assertion that Soviet regimes do in fact act for the interests of the many, for, if the mere claim to act for those interests is sufficient to establish democratic legitimacy, hardly any regime would fail the test. Moreover, Macpherson's view that democracy meant originally 'rule by or in the interests of the hitherto oppressed class' is doubtful. It would be a truer account of the fundamental assumptions behind traditional discussions of democracy to say that it has meant rule by *and therefore* in the interests of the poor. Aristotle's definition of democracy as the government of the poor was the conclusion of a syllogism: democracy is the rule of the many, in all countries the many are poor and the few are rich, therefore democracy is the rule of the poor. As we have seen, this syllogism may now in certain circumstances be inapplicable since its second premise may be untrue, and we may therefore be faced with the problem of oppressed poor minorities. Nevertheless, it has been common in the past to both defenders and critics that democratic rule would lead to government in the interests of the poor or at least in accordance with the wishes of the poor. The qualification is significant, for in the main it has been critics of democracy who have made it. Whilst democratic rule would be rule in accordance with the wishes of the poor, it would not be in the interests of those incapable of understanding their true interests. Therefore, argued say a Macaulay, democracy should be avoided and government left to those who can appreciate and act on the real interests of the community. It is difficult to see how the Leninist position differs, except possibly in a reluctance to abandon the ideological prestige of democracy. To divorce the term democracy entirely from a political context and to confine it to the social sphere is to drain it of meaning. Democracy has to do with equality, as Macpherson says, but it has to do primarily with political equality, equality of influence over political decision-making. It may be that such equality is inevitably lessened by inequalities in other areas, in income, in education, in access to the means of communication. But the eradication of such inequalities (supposing that this is what Soviet regimes have achieved) does not automatically create political equality, if a ruling elite can maintain itself without any reference or accountability to the people. If social inequalities can only be destroyed, and if 'alienation' and 'dehumanization' can only be overcome, by elite rule, the sacrifice of democracy may be worth while. It makes little sense to deny that any sacrifice is being made. We can conclude that merely for a government to act in the interests of the ruled is not sufficient for it to be a democracy.

Is it sufficient if the rulers are chosen by the ruled or their representatives? Again this is the case that has been put forward recently, although by apologists of a different political complexion. Let us take the example of Schumpeter who, in his *Capitalism, Socialism and Democracy*, set out what he claimed to be a new theory of democracy. Whatever its novelty, it has certainly been an influential theory. Schumpeter's answer to the question at issue here, how the people can rule, was straightforward. Small primitive communities, in which face-to-face relations prevail and political issues are simple, can conceivably allow for popular participation in the duties of legislation and administration. In no other instance can the people be said to rule, except by a confusing redefinition of the word. To settle what the role of the people can and should be, Schumpeter examined what he took to be the then prevailing classical theory of democracy. This doctrine understood the democratic method as 'that institutional arrangement for arriving at political decisions which realizes the common good by making the people itself decide issues through the election of individuals who are to assemble in order to carry out its will'.[14] Schumpeter poses two main criticisms of the doctrine, firstly that there does not and cannot exist any common will towards a common good, and secondly that the ordinary citizen is not competent to fill the role demanded of him by the theory. There is no determinate common good on which all men can agree. The problem is not just that men are irrational or that they may take as their ends objectives other than the common good. It is also that views of the common good are related to ultimate ends which are beyond the compass of rational argument. Even if a consensus on these ultimate values were reached, there might still be wide disagreement on how to apply these generalities to particular issues. If there can be no agreement within these two areas, there can be no common will of the kind postulated by the classical theory. In addition, the ordinary citizen is peculiarly ill-suited to making political decisions. The classical doctrine presupposes that he has an independent and definite will in the political sphere. All the evidence goes to show that this assumption is mistaken and that human behaviour is heavily affected by extra-rational and irrational factors. Even the economists have found that their assumption of the rational consumer can be false, particularly in face of advertising. Nevertheless the economic consumer lives in a world of everyday experience and brings to his small-scale decisions some sense of reality and some feeling of responsibility. In the field of politics, where the ordinary citizen is inexperienced and his judgement is not disciplined by consideration of the consequences to himself of his own actions, this sense of reality and assumption of responsibility disappears and the ordinary man yields to prejudice and impulse. Freed of the moral constraints and the claims of circumstances restricting him in private life, he is open to the artifices of those groups who wish to fashion or manipulate his attitudes. Even more than the economic consumer in the economic sphere, the ordinary political man is the product of the political process rather than its generator.

[14] Joseph A. Schumpeter, *Capitalism, Socialism and Democracy* (London, 4th ed., 1952), p. 250.

In view of these supposed defects in the classical theory, Schumpeter offers a redefinition of democracy moving the emphasis away from the electorate's function of deciding on issues towards its function of producing a government. On this new definition, 'the democratic method is that institutional arrangement for arriving at political decisions in which individuals acquire the power to decide by means of a competitive struggle for the people's vote'.[15] In other words, in terms of the categories listed at the beginning of this section, Schumpeter wished to claim that the fulfilling of the sixth or seventh requirements, that rulers should be chosen by the ruled or their representatives, is sufficient for a system to be democratic.

There is some ambiguity about the status of this new theory of democracy. Although Schumpeter claims for it that it is 'much truer to life' a good deal of his argument is directed towards demonstrating the desirability of a system conforming to his definition rather than demonstrating its descriptive propriety. For instance, even if all that Schumpeter says about the incompetence of the ordinary citizen is true, this would amount only to a good case against allowing men-in-the-street to decide on issues, not to a proof that no system could possibly assign such a role to them. The considerable normative component in the discussion is shown most clearly when he turns to the conditions necessary to a successful democracy. Politicians should be drawn from a social class traditionally associated with ruling. Democratic governments should be informed, even instructed, by a bureaucracy imbued with a strong sense of duty and *esprit de corps*, qualities which again can best be guaranteed by drawing civil servants from a social class 'of adequate quality and corresponding prestige'. The democratic voter must respect the political division of labour by leaving decisions on issues to the leaders whom they have elected.[16] Although value objections might be put to this vision of an ideal polity in which the people keep to their political station, no methodological objection could be raised if it was acknowledged to be a statement of an ideal. Such objections are perfectly legitimate when the ideal is claimed to have some greater scientific purchase than others and when it appropriates the word democracy to describe itself.

[15] Ibid., p. 269.   [16] Ibid., pp. 290–5.

Nevertheless, it could be argued, this new definition of democracy has the merit of conforming, in a way that the classical doctrine does not, to the realities of liberal democracies. Of course, even if this is true, it does not follow from the fact that 'classical' democracy does not exist that it cannot ever exist; nor does it force us to redefine democracy, for it might just as well lead us to the conclusion that Western systems are not democracies or are only imperfect democracies. The prior question is, however, whether or not the new theory is more realistic. Can elections in liberal democracies be seen simply as a choice of the leading man or men and not as popular decisions on issues? Once this question is answered, we can turn to the other question of how far a political system satisfying this sole requirement could be regarded as democratic.

Schumpeter stresses the parallel between the market economy and democratic politics, quoting with approval the American politician's remark: 'What businessmen do not understand is that exactly as they are dealing in oil so I am dealing in votes.'[17] Politicians act to maximize votes, just as economic entrepreneurs act to maximize profits. Now this assumption, combined with the complementary assumption that voters act in order to maximize their interests, can be the basis of fruitful if limited theories of democracy resembling in structure economic theories. Schumpeter, however, abandons the market economy analogy by refusing to allow the second assumption.[18] Whilst the politician is pictured as an entrepreneur, it is not clear what he is selling, or indeed if he is selling anything. To put this another way, Schumpeter is unwilling to admit any degree of consumer sovereignty in democratic politics, since this would be to admit the possibility of the political consumer, the voter, choosing between the goods offered by the politicians, different policies or different performances in office.

The only reason given for this departure from the market

[17] Ibid., p. 285.

[18] See below, Chapter Three, section 3. That parts of Schumpeter's analysis actually run counter to 'economic' theories of democracy is a fact not appreciated even by those who have been foremost in elaborating them. See Anthony Downs, *An Economic Theory of Democracy* (New York, 1957, paperback ed.), p. 29, footnote 11.

analogy is the inefficacy of commercial advertising in comparison with political propaganda. The prettiest girl is not able for long to sell a bad cigarette (bad presumably in terms of the wishes and tastes of the consumer); but, we are told, there is no such resistance to persuasion, no such consumer discrimination, in the political market. Now it seems at least as plausible an assumption that politicians try to present policies they believe the electorate (or sections of it) want as that they command the ability to fashion the electorate's attitude to fit them to whatever may be on offer. Nevertheless, even if the manipulation of popular opinions were as fine an art as Schumpeter supposes, this still would not mean that elections are not decisions on issues but merely a choice of persons.

It is somewhat difficult to understand what can be meant by claiming that it is 'the primary function of the electorate to produce a government' rather than to decide issues. Does this mean that competing parties cannot disagree on policy questions? The claim is unconvincing. Whatever the means by which the politician maximizes his voting profits (whether by providing what the voter wants or by getting the voter to want his particular product), it is difficult to see how in a competitive situation the choice offered can always be simply that of persons. For the fact of competition between groups aspiring to leadership will at least allow different groups to attach themselves to different policy positions. Whatever the skill possessed by the winning group, whether skill in seeing what the people want or in manipulating their wants, the choice of one group rather than another can imply the choice of one set of policies rather than another. In this sense, elections can certainly decide issues.

Does the claim that the primary function of the electorate is to produce a government mean then that the consideration of 'issues' never determines the voters' choice? Again the claim is implausible. A preference for one party rather than another can hardly be divorced from beliefs about what the party stands for or expectations about how it will act if it forms a government. There may be various grounds for these expectations—promises made by the parties, their past performances in office or their general ideological stances. There may be various motives inspiring voters' preferences—self-interest, prejudice or general ideological commitment. Even if a voter's expectations are quite unreal, even if he is unaware in detail of the policy differences between parties, even if he is dominated in his choice by prejudice or impulse, his vote may still be decided by a preference for one sort of government or set of policies rather than another.

It could nevertheless be argued that, though competing parties can disagree on issues and the electorate can choose on the basis of issues rather than persons, it does not follow that the electorate decides policies in the sense that their preferences determine government actions. On this view, the fact that issues are raised in electoral campaigns does not result in any control over governmental policy after the elections. Again this is implausible, since it would imply that governments can safely and habitually ignore their election promises and can decide on current issues without any consideration of electoral repercussions. If, as seems more plausible, competing individuals or parties take up positions they suppose will attract support and if governments take into account the electoral effects of their acts, the democratic method does empirically allow for some control by the ruled over the policies of rulers. In this case Schumpeter's new definition of the democratic method certainly seems no 'truer to life' than older definitions which have seen it as a method by which rulers are made accountable to and controllable by the ruled.

Whether or not Schumpeter's redefinition is true to the life of Western democracies, it is still an understandable, defensible and not altogether novel position that, since ordinary men are incompetent, they should not be given the power to decide political issues. The novelty lies in trying to reconcile this view with a democratic norm. As we have already seen, it would be difficult to know what criterion could be used to define and defend a wide extension of citizenship unless competence to decide *some* questions is assumed to be an attribute of the ordinary man. We have seen too that Schumpeter's definition is not a 'realistic' definition in the sense that it fits easily with the practice of Western democracies. We might ask in addition if any system which did conform to the new definition could be called democratic. In terms of our original categories, can a system which neither includes a direct participatory element nor allows for accountability of rulers to ruled be called democratic? One fact that suggests otherwise is the expectation that in representative democracies there should be not only elections but periodic elections. Imagine a system in which a king is elected for life. So long as there is competition for the office, such a regime would seem to satisfy Schumpeter's requirement for democracy. If the point of elections is simply to authorize independent decision-makers and not to affect government outputs, no stipulations about periodicity or frequency of elections are necessary. All that would be necessary would be a rule about the election of a new king when the old king needed replacement because of death or incapacity. We require elections at or within fixed periods presumably in order to ensure that some control can be exercised over the actions of governments by the electorate. Another expectation of a democratic system that goes beyond Schumpeter's definition is that there should be at least the possibility of competition between candidates of different political or social standpoints. Schumpeter does assume that, in principle at least, everyone should be free in a democracy to compete for leadership by presenting themselves as candidates.[19] This freedom is not, however, entailed by his definition. Let us imagine another system, like for instance the present system in Poland, where there are representative bodies and competition for places in them, in the sense that there are more candidates than seats, but in which candidates have to be approved by a single political party. This also seems to satisfy Schumpeter's requirement: voters have a choice of persons even though, owing partly at least to the lack of any choice between political positions, this may not enable them to affect in even a general way the decisions of government. Again such a system would not count as democratic because this deficiency prevents any governmental accountability being established. It is not then a sufficient condition of a democracy that rulers be chosen by the ruled or their representatives. There must be in addition some accountability of rulers to the ruled or their representatives. This is not of course to deny that for rulers to be accountable they must be chosen by the ruled or their representatives.

[19] Not apparently in practice since he does not accept that 'unfair' or 'fraudulent' competition or restraint of competition would disqualify a system as democratic. See op. cit., pp. 271–2.

Although they arise from very different preoccupations, the arguments presented by Macpherson and Schumpeter, what might be labelled the communist and elitist views of democracy, have some assumptions in common. Firstly, they share a minimal concept of democracy; that is to say, both require very little by way of popular involvement and no or very little satisfaction of the claims of equality for a system to be democratic. Secondly, this minimal concept is based in both cases on a distrust of the masses, a belief that the ordinary man is incapable, in the one case of correctly understanding his own real interests, in the other of making any kind of competent judgement in political matters. What has been argued here is not that these assumptions are necessarily wrong but that they are impossible to fit into a democratic frame, and that the minimal requirements posed by the communist and elitist arguments are insufficient, even if satisfied, to constitute democracy, the rule of the people.

Responsible government

In terms of our original statement of possible requirements, one or more of the first four requirements must be satisfied for a system to be democratic. These requirements can be regrouped into two broader and more traditional categories, direct democracy—systems that satisfy either of the first two requirements —and responsible government—those that satisfy one of the other two requirements.

The institutions necessary for direct democracy are obvious; those necessary for responsible government less so. For responsible government to exist some control must be exercisable by the electorate over the actions of government. The exact degree of control that is desirable, in view of the many demands that we might make of government other than that it be democratic, has traditionally been a matter of debate, fought out in such questions as whether or not a government needs a mandate for major policy initiatives and whether a representative is merely a spokesman for his constituents' views or should exercise some independence of judgement. Nevertheless, the traditional assumption has been that some popular control over governmental decisions is a necessary feature; it has been left to recent democratic revision-ists to suggest that democracy is compatible with the absence of such control. In fact, their provision of responsible government constitutes the securest justification liberal democracies have for their self-description.

What then are the conditions necessary for the existence of responsible government? What is needed to ensure that some popular control can be exerted over political leadership, some governmental accountability can be enforced? Two main con-ditions can be suggested, that governments should be removable by electoral decisions and that some alternative can be substituted by electoral decision. The alternative, it should be stressed, must be more than an alternative governing group. It must compre-hend alternatives in policy, since it is only if an electoral decision can alter the actions of government that popular control can be said to be established. The power of replacing Tweedledum by Tweedledee (the 'Ins' by the 'Outs', as Bentham had it) would be an insufficient basis for such control. To borrow the economic analogy, competition is meaningless, or at any rate cannot create consumer sovereignty, unless there is some product differentiation.

In detail there might be a great deal of discussion about the institutional arrangements necessary to responsible government, but in general some are obvious. There must be free elections, in which neither the incumbent government nor any other group can determine the electoral result by means other than indications of how they will act if returned to power. Fraud, intimidation and bribery are thus incompatible with responsible government. Monetary bribery in elections, it might be said, is in principle no different from and might indeed have no worse consequences than promises to the electorate or sections of it to pursue policies favourable to their interests or prejudices. Morally this might be the case; and it might also be true that, if offered the opportunity, many voters would accept bribes (half a guinea Bentham believed would pervert a vote). The defence of laws excluding bribery as an electoral tactic cannot be solely that bribery is immoral unless, as is certainly possible, this is coupled with condemnation of any consideration of private interests by the voter in casting his vote. The alternative defence is simply that it would militate against accountability. Another part of the institutional frame necessary

D

to responsible government is freedom of association. Unless groups wishing to compete for leadership have the freedom to organize and formulate alternative programmes, the presentation of alternatives would be impossible. Lastly, freedom of speech is necessary since silent alternatives can never be effective alternatives. In considering such arrangements, we cannot stick at simple legal considerations; we must move from questions of 'freedom from' to questions of 'ability to'. The absence of any legal bar to association will not, for example, create the ability to associate if there are heavy costs involved which only some groups can bear. Nor will the legal guarantee of freedom of speech be of much use if access to the mass media is severely restricted.

This could be summed up by saying that responsible government depends largely upon the existence of, and free competition between, political parties. The point is not just that competing parties will be an inevitable consequence of the kind of institutional arrangements we have been discussing. It is that it is largely through parties that coherent alternatives can be presented to a wide electorate and the voter can discern some relation between his vote and possible government action. The degree to which parties alone can perform these functions will vary with the type of governmental system. Where the elective element is confined to the election of a single individual as leader (let us call this a presidential system), parties might not be necessary to perform the function of creating coherent alternatives, since the individual candidates can do this. This is not to say, of course, that in a purely presidential system parties would not emerge, since their purpose from the politicians' point of view is to assemble and organize the vote rather than to construct policies and impose them uniformly. Where the election is not of a single individual as leader but of a number of representatives of different areas or groups within a community (let us call this an assembly system), the creation of coherent alternatives depends upon organized parties. Since a presidential system would be rendered more continuously accountable by the presence of a representative assembly with some control over the elected leader, parties are a necessary feature of responsible government.

How far can different types of party system reinforce or weaken responsible government? To take one obvious dimension, are one-party, two-party, or multi-party systems equally conducive to accountability?

From what has been said, it would seem that a one-party system is incompatible with responsible government since it does not allow for the creation of coherent alternatives. This is true; or, at the least, a one-party system allowing for this would be virtually indistinguishable from a two- or a multi-party system. What would be necessary for a one-party state to qualify as democratic? In the first place, the party would have to be completely open and comprehensive. No individual or group could be excluded from membership and no political viewpoint denied expression within it. The party would have to be perfectly eclectic in terms of both persons and opinions. Secondly, factionalism would have to be allowed within the party. In other words, groups within the party would need to be free to organize themselves and to press their policies within it. Thirdly, unless membership of the party was coterminous with a democratic electorate, these different groups would have to be capable of presenting different candidates in extra-party elections. For otherwise the leadership would be responsible only to party members and not to all competent citizens.[20] In general, for a one-party system to allow for responsible government, the party would have either to become simply the community acting in its electoral role or to tolerate a degree of internal division extending to mutual opposition in extra-party elections. In either case, something very like a two-party or a multi-party system would be present.

We are left with the comparison between two- and multi-party systems. It has often been claimed for two-party systems that they reinforce governmental accountability by presenting the voter

[20] These requirements are more stringent than those posed by C. B. Macpherson when he asks how the Communist 'Vanguard State' could become democratic in a 'narrow sense'. He stipulates only that there should be full intra-party democracy, that party membership should be open and that membership should not require a degree of activity beyond the capacity of the average person (op. cit., pp. 20–1). He does not say what would be necessary for 'full intra-party democracy'. Even if control by those at the bottom of the party was established, this would still only create accountability of the leadership to party members; whether this could count as democratic would depend on the extent of party membership.

with clear-cut alternatives, enabling him to see a direct relation between his vote and the actions of any potential government. The issue is not quite so straightforward, however, since there may be processes within such a system which obscure or narrow the alternatives between which the voter can choose. Clearly, in a two-party system, he has a clear choice between two sets of potential leaders. So far as his judgement of the possible future actions of the parties in office is based on an assessment of the characters of party leaders, he can hope to determine future government action since he can certainly hope to affect which set of leaders is put into power.

In many circumstances, however, a two-party system may narrow or eliminate the alternatives presented to voters by bringing the parties close together in terms of policy positions. It is commonplace to remark on the fact that, in a two-party system, the parties tend to contest the middle ground and reduce the ideological and programmatic distance between themselves. It is easy to see why this should be so. Assuming that parties adopt policies which they think will win elections, they will (unless their judgements of the actual situation are widely different) take up positions close to each other; for only one position can win. The tendency is clear if most voters are distributed symmetrically around some one point on the political spectrum. Any party which moves away from that single pole will allow the other party to move with it and capture a winning majority. In consequence, both parties will tend to move to the central polar position. This tendency will be present even under different distributions within the electorate. Suppose that, in their political positions, voters are evenly spread along a spectrum. For either party to move away from the centre of the spectrum is a losing strategy if the opposing party moves in the same direction. The tendency again holds even if there is a bimodal distribution of opinion in the electorate. If a party sticks at the modal point representing the maximum of its support, it leaves open the possibility of the opposition moving towards a centre which, although perhaps comparatively sparsely populated, could constitute an election-winning margin. Thus both parties will tend to move away from the central position of their support towards the central position of the whole electorate. Only where the electorate is polarized at the extremes might parties be inhibited from moving towards the centre by the fear of the bulk of their supporters abstaining or even creating new extreme parties.[21] But this is in any case a situation in which there is unlikely to be a sufficient degree of consensus to sustain a system of responsible government. Therefore, given the kinds of distribution of opinion which can make a democratic system possible at all, there will be a tendency for parties in a two-party system to take up ideological and programmatic positions close to one another.

Of course, there may be some countervailing factors restricting the ability of parties to act with the degree of flexibility this analysis assumes. Politicians themselves may have ideological commitments which they cannot easily abandon or alter. Parties may draw their organizational strength from voluntary activists whose continued support depends upon broad adherence to some determinate ideological positions. Parties may suffer electorally in the long run if they pursue electoral advantage with too little principle. Nevertheless, there may be a pressure towards the elimination of ideological and programmatic differentials between parties in a two-party system and, to the degree that these differences diminish, the possibility of responsible government recedes. It has often enough been stated that some consensus between parties is necessary to the stability of democracy. It needs also to be remembered that lack of party differentiation reduces governmental accountability to the electorate. The point is not just that the absence of party differences might lead to popular apathy and even disillusion with the democratic system, but that it makes it logically impossible for electoral decisions to affect actions of government. 'The end of ideology' might be welcomed on other grounds, but it can hardly enhance the prospects of responsible government.

The same pressures towards conformity do not operate in a

[21] In his analysis of the effects of distribution of voters in two-party systems, Anthony Downs considers a bimodal distribution with the modes near each extreme as the only alternative to a unimodal, symmetrical distribution, and puts the argument that, in this type of bimodal distribution, the parties will maintain their ideological distance (op. cit., pp. 117–20). He does not consider a bimodal distribution where the modes are not at the extreme.

multi-party system. Such a system will probably be the result of a multimodal distribution of political positions within the electorate, or of a situation where there is bipolarization of opinions on a number of cross-cutting issues. Given the existence of a multi-party system, there will be no incentive for parties to congregate around the same policy positions and every incentive for them to stand clearly in the ideological space occupied by their supporters. Any move by a party to its right or left will create the risk of the party to its left or right capturing its 'own' supporters.[22] Thus in a multi-party system, parties will tend to maintain and stress their ideological and programmatic distinctiveness. In terms of our present discussion, this does allow them to present to the electorate a clear choice of policy alternatives. In this, it has the advantage over a two-party system. From another viewpoint, it is at a disadvantage. The prime virtue of a two-party system as a means of enforcing accountability is that it presents a clear relationship between electoral decisions and government actions. Government accountability is easily translated into party responsibility since, in normal circumstances, only one party controls government and the election decides which. The voter, in deciding for the party of his choice, is deciding also for the government of his choice. In a multi-party system, it is less probable that a single party will win control of government (except of course in a presidential election) and less easy therefore for the voter to attribute responsibility for government actions to particular parties. It is difficult for the voter to judge between parties on the basis of past performances, since, even if a party has participated in a government, it can disclaim responsibility for particular policies of that government. It is equally difficult for the voter to judge on the basis of particular policy positions, since, even if a party does participate in government after the election, there is no guarantee that its policies will survive the necessary compromise of coalitions. Thus the voter will probably choose on the basis of the general ideological stances of the parties. In itself this does not distinguish him from the voter in a two-party system, who might rationally use party ideologies as a basis of choice. The

[22] The necessarily static stance of parties is not affected if we are thinking, not of a multimodal distribution along one dimension, but of a two-dimensional distribution across a plane.

difference is that the voter in a two-party system can use party ideologies as indications of the way in which governments are likely to act, the voter in a multi-party system cannot. He will probably be voting for what a party says rather than for what it has done or can be expected to do. And, as words are cheaper than deeds, this is a situation in which the enforcement of accountability is difficult.

There are then severe problems in posing the conditions of responsible government. It requires that citizens be able to choose between alternative governmental policies. This in turn requires the existence of competing parties (or, if this means anything different, freely competing groups within a one-party system). Different party systems have different disadvantages from the point of view of accountability. What can be said is that the optimal conditions are likely to exist where there is a two-party system in which some ideological distance is maintained between the parties or a multi-party system in which stable coalitions are the norm. In the first case there is a clear relation between party choice and government action together with some real choice as between parties. In the second case, there is a real choice between parties together with some assurance about the government formations in which a particular party will participate.

3. CONCLUSION

The perhaps disappointing conclusion is that it is impossible to define democracy in any very concrete institutional terms. Certainly it is impossible to identify democracy absolutely with majority decision although in most instances this might be the method of taking decisions most conducive to democracy. In examining the notion of 'the people' and the notion of 'rule', we have seen that in different circumstances different operational rules might be needed to reach the maximum of democracy achievable in those circumstances. We cannot therefore define democracy in terms of particular institutions or methods but only in terms of the ends which are to be maximized.

What, in summary, are these ends? Remembering the definition of a citizen as one who takes part in political decision-making, one basic democratic norm is that all should be citizens, or at any rate that very clear evidence of personal incapacity must be produced to justify deprivation of citizenship. Another is that there should be equality between citizens in their capacity to determine decisions.

Clearly this second end is incapable of full achievement. Even in the best of all possible democratic worlds, the urge to participate in public affairs might be stronger in some than in others. Discounting personal tastes, there will always be other barriers to political equality. In the first place, no decision-making procedure can ensure that all will always determine decisions. In all the cases where such a procedure is really needed, that is in the instances where there is disagreement about what the decision should be, equality in determining the decision is impossible. The most that can be asked of the procedures is that they should ensure that everyone's chances of determining decisions are as high as possible whilst no one person's or group's chances are persistently less than those of the rest. The arrangements that will satisfy this dual requirement will be contingent upon circumstances, particularly on whether or not a permanent minority exists.

A second barrier to political equality is the necessity for some political division of labour. Even in the smallest community, it might be necessary, if only to save on expenditure of time and energy, to delegate the responsibility for some decision-making to particular persons or groups. The inequalities so created might be lessened by a greater involvement of the ordinary citizen in crucial decision-making or in administrative duties; they might be mitigated either by subjecting ruling groups directly to popular control or by restricting them to actions within rules (laws) decided by the people. They could not be eradicated by such devices.

Thirdly, political inequalities may derive from inequalities in other areas. This might be one good argument for reducing those inequalities. On the other hand, some of the inequalities that give rise to political differentiation may be beyond our power to alter. If, for example, differences of intelligence (or at any rate political skills) are partially the product of genetic endowment, the political inequalities resulting from such differences are impossible, at least for the moment, to remove. It may be too that the eradication of these inequalities, even if possible, would be undesirable. Supposing genetic engineering could make uniform our inherited endowment, it might not be a sufficient reason to utilize it that this would enhance political equality. More immediately, there may be good reasons for maintaining income differentials or the influence of the family upon the child even whilst acknowledging that differences in income or family background may breed political inequalities. This is to say no more than that democratic norms must compete with other social ends that we may hold to be good.

Although democratic norms cannot be wholly fulfilled, or could be wholly fulfilled only at the cost of sacrifices few would care to make, this does not mean they are useless in judging or defining political systems. In normative terms, political systems are better or worse to the degree that these ends are satisfied. In definitional terms, systems are more or less democratic to the degree that these norms are realized.

Whilst no one set of institutional arrangements can be labelled as democratic, the term is not infinitely malleable. Axiomatically, no system which debars the mass of non-rulers from playing any part in the process of decision-making can be deemed democratic; and no 'definition' of democracy that excludes such a role is tenable. Nevertheless, there are different requirements which, if satisfied, can allow popular participation in the decision-making process. Broadly, these requirements can be identified with either direct democracy or responsible government. More specifically, we can isolate three criteria by which the degree of democracy in any community may be tested—firstly the extent to which all constituent groups are incorporated into the decision-making processes, or negatively the extent to which some groups are excluded from or under-endowed with political influence; secondly, the extent to which governmental decisions are subject to popular control, the extent that is of responsible government; thirdly, the degree to which ordinary citizens are involved in public administration, the extent that is of the experience of ruling and being ruled.

Three

THEORIES OF DEMOCRACY

Clearly a definition of democracy is only the beginning of discussion. A number of further questions immediately arise. How do democracies work? What advantages do they have, what social ends do they serve other than political equality? These questions are by no means distinct. To know what ends democracies might serve, we must have some idea of how they work or would work. To explain how a political system works, we must have in mind some notion of the standards against which its performance is to be measured. Nevertheless, by an act of rough surgery, this chapter will deal largely with the first question and the next chapter with the second.

Here, a distinction will be made between the types of theory that have been utilized in discussion of democracy. At the risk of over-simplification, we can distinguish four different types: classifications (or ideal types); empirical generalizations; deductive models; and utopian schemes. The risk should be stressed. In the first place, it is doubtful if the term 'theory' can properly or at any rate usefully be applied in common to all these modes of discussing democracy. In the second place, it is unlikely that anyone writing on democracy will confine himself to one mode of discussion; indeed, it might not be possible for him to do so.

1. CLASSIFICATION OR IDEAL TYPES

One of the first but most persistent tasks that presents itself in any field of thought is to invent, refine or systematize a vocabulary. Until we have words and concepts which enable us to define and distinguish phenomena, the real world must remain shapeless, indescribable and thus inexplicable. We cannot understand the real world without understanding and developing the words and concepts we use to describe it. In much of the study of politics, this refinement and development must be concerned with the elaboration of classificatory systems or typologies enabling us to group together and distinguish political systems or elements within them. Essential to the construction of such typologies is a statement of the particular dimension or dimensions to be treated and a clear definition of the classes along this continuum. Clearly such elaboration of 'ideal types' can only be usefully done by those acquainted with the real world they aim to describe, for typologies are useless if they do not fit even approximately any real phenomena. Equally clearly, the exercise is not just empirical description (still less scientific hypothesizing) for the ideal types are conceptual constructs which may have no clear or exact counterparts in the real world. Weber, who coined the phrase and understood the strengths and limitations of the method, did not suppose that his ideal types of authority—'traditional', 'rational-legal' and 'charismatic'—would fit with one-to-one exactitude any actual authority structures.

The phrase may be comparatively recent, the method is much older. Its oldest application has been in typologies classifying political systems, or elements within them, according to different distributions of power through the trilogy of monarchy, aristocracy and democracy. Again, it should be stressed, it has seldom been supposed that these ideal types actually do or could occur in pure forms. Where the words have been applied to actual systems, this is because those systems approximated most closely to the ideal type. Indeed, not only has it been thought 'mixed' systems were possible, there has been a long tradition approving of such mixed government, a tradition which (it will be argued) has persisted largely unrecognized into much present-day discussion of democracy.

It would go far beyond the limits of this book to trace the history of this typology, which has been the common coin of political discussion from the Greeks to the nineteenth century. Thinkers as distant in time, although as comparable in influence, as Aristotle and Montesquieu have found in it a basic tool for political analysis. For both, the statement of the typology was only the beginning of exploration. Broadly, aside from the initial classification, they were concerned with three major areas of discussion: what are the environmental conditions which will foster and sustain different political systems; how do different systems work; what are their respective merits and demerits. It is salutary to remember that they did look at the first, since a concern with the social substructure of politics is often thought, on all political wings, to be the crowning glory of modern political science. In the second area, their methods were largely intuitive and historical; that is to say they reached their conclusions about how systems work by the accumulation of historical examples and anecdotal illustrations. Lastly, their concern with evaluating the merits of different systems was unashamed, quite unhampered by the 'value-free' diffidence of modern social scientists.

The long-serving typology of monarchy, aristocracy and democracy has suffered a decline in recent years, perhaps because historically the rule of the one has been closely associated with hereditary monarchs and the rule of the few with dukes. Nevertheless, there has been at least one strenuous attempt to construct an 'ideal type' of democracy, by Robert Dahl, in his *Preface to Democratic Theory*.[1] We have already examined Dahl's definition of polyarchy as 'minorities government'; here we are concerned mainly with his methodology. He does not use the phrase 'ideal type' but talks of 'maximising' theory. Such a theory is one which stipulates the goals or values to be achieved and seeks to establish the conditions necessary to their achievement. The goals to be achieved by democracy or polyarchal democracy are political

---

[1] The argument here is contained largely in Chapter 3, pp. 63–89.

equality and popular sovereignty.[2] Dahl deduces those institutional conditions which are logically necessary to the full attainment of democratic goals. During the voting period all should
express a preference between alternatives, for instance by voting,
the weight of each person's vote should be equal and the winning
alternative should be that with the greatest number of votes.
Before the vote, anyone should be able to insert an alternative
he prefers more than those presently available and all should be
equally informed about the alternative. After the vote, alternatives with the greatest number of votes should displace those with
fewer and the orders of elected officials should be followed.
Between elections, all decisions should be either mandated in the
election or mandated in some other way (presumably by referendum) or both. No organization has ever fulfilled, or is ever
likely to fulfil these conditions, but those approximating most
closely to them can be classed as 'polyarchies'. The question
next arises of what conditions in the real world are necessary for
the existence of polyarchy. Dahl suggests a number, mostly to do
with agreement on these conditions considered as norms and with
the social training necessary to create or sustain such consensus.

Dahl admits that there is little that is novel in this type of
argument, and there is no need to dispute his judgement.[3] In
particular, there is little that is new in the methodology, for the
maximizing theory of democracy is no more than the construction of ideal types which we can meet with in Aristotle or Montesquieu. Two parallels might be especially stressed. In the first
place, the theory is not an empirical theory in the sense that it is
productive of empirical hypotheses. It utilizes rather than gives
rise to such hypotheses, and in this Dahl is no different from
Aristotle or Montesquieu. His statement of the conditions necessary to sustain polyarchy are not suggested relationships which
empirical researchers can test, but are derived from his own
knowledge of the empirical evidence on the links between belief
in democratic norms and democratic stability, or between the

[2] These are stipulated by Dahl as the goals of 'populistic' democracy.
Although he does not state them explicitly as the goals of polyarchal democracy, his discussion presupposes that the goals are common.

[3] Op. cit., p. 82. Nor would one wish to dispute Dahl's claim that his
argument is set out more rigorously than is customary.

prevalence of democratic norms and the type of social training received in the family, the schools and so on. The evidence we have now available on political behaviour may be greater and more systematic than that available to Aristotle or Montesquieu. Dahl's discussion, however, stands in no different relationship to that evidence. Like his predecessors, he is calling on experience to give body to his typological definition.

The second parallel is that, except possibly in a trivial sense, Dahl's discussion is not value-free. The trivial way in which a discussion of democracy could be value-free would be if the writer refused to commit himself to any personal preferences. In fact, Dahl reveals unmistakably that he believes what he calls 'the American hybrid' to have great merit. More importantly, his maximizing theory starts from a definition of democratic goals and the conditions logically necessary to achieve them. His subsequent strategy is to ask what social preconditions are present when those conditions are approximately reached in real-world polyarchies. No different structure of argument would have been needed if he had asked instead what social preconditions would be necessary for those logically necessary conditions to be more fully achieved, even in real-world polyarchies. In other words, the 'maximizing theory' would not alter in form if the conditions were used as ends of action rather than as measuring rods against which existing systems can be graded. It could be as useful to the political engineer as to the political investigator.

Perhaps the greatest drawback of Dahl's discussion, compared to that of his predecessors, is that it is largely the construction of a class of one. If the major point of typologies is to enrich our vocabulary, we need to isolate more than one point along a continuum. Admittedly, Dahl does suggest that a classification could be constructed according to the proximity of systems to the democractic ideal type; the classification he suggests, distinguishing egalitarian polyarchies, non-egalitarian polyarchies, oligarchies, dictatorships and mixed polities, falls squarely into a traditional pattern.[4] However, this suggestion is relegated to a short appendix.

[4] Ibid., p. 87. More recently, in his book *Polyarchy* (Yale, 1971), he has put forward a four-fold distinction between closed hegemonies, inclusive hegemonies, competitive oligarchies and polyarchies. This is a classifica-

This shortcoming merely exemplifies a general confusion of contrasts. Whatever the reason for the decline of the old classification, whether because it has a musty odour or because apologists of every political shade wish to appropriate the prestige of democracy, it has become difficult to know with what democracy is to be compared. The loss of clarity in the classifications we use results in obscurity in our political thinking. Two brief illustrations of this obfuscation can be given. One distinction frequently drawn, though difficult to sustain, is between democratic and totalitarian systems. An important part of any definition of totalitarianism must be to do with the extent of governmental control over individual behaviour and thought, and presumably the class from which it is to be distinguished is 'liberalism' or 'limited government'. The opposition of totalitarianism and democracy suggests some necessary connection between democracy and limited government, and this connection might not always hold.[5] The root difficulty is that this particular contrast confuses two dimensions. Democracy is to do essentially with the locus of power, totalitarianism with its extent; the contraposing of the two is bound to lead to confusion.

The confusion of contrasts shows even more clearly in the debate on the elite theory of democracy. The early elite theorists, writers such as Mosca and Pareto, were concerned not to reconstruct democratic theory but to demolish the base on which it rested, the assumption that political power could be differentially distributed. Significantly, they attacked the older typologies of Aristotle and Montesquieu as myths, illusions which have hidden a reality common to all political systems. Whatever the formal structure, power is always wielded by a small minority, a ruling group taking the most important decisions and beyond the control of the majority. No constitutional mechanism can reduce, although it may obscure, the oligarchic structure of politics. Clearly, if this is true and if there are no differences between societies in the independence which ruling groups enjoy, any typology based on the dimension of the distribution of power

tion along two dimensions, the degree to which there is political competition and the degree to which the opportunity to participate is extended to all.

[5] See below Chapter Four, section 3.

and any theory of democracy based on the notions of rule by or responsibility to the people would be meaningless. Despite this, there have been attempts to incorporate elitist ideas into a democratic frame. We have already considered one such attempt in Schumpeter's redefinition of democracy. It is implicit in his argument that what distinguishes a democracy is not that all or most make decisions. 'Democracies', like other systems, are ruled by small numbers. Nor presumably are they to be distinguished by the existence of competition between elites, since the Yorkists and the Lancastrians, the Guelphs and the Ghibellines, also competed. What does distinguish democracy is a particular procedure for deciding who is the victor, an alternative to methods such as battle or the hereditary principle. Schumpeter was thinking solely in terms of competition between politicians. More recently, the terms have been widened to include a greater plurality of elites. On this view, what characterizes democracy is that there is a diffusion of political influence amongst a large number of power sources. The power of politicians, the power they wield that is by the incumbency of office, is only one of the faces of power. Control over economic resources may be another. More particularly, influence over political decisions is diffused over a host of organized groups—trade unions, business organizations, churches, societies for the promotion of this or the protection of that—which express a variety of views and interests. The existence of different forms of power and the presence of a complex of organizations mediating between the citizen and the state make up an effective system of checks and balances limiting the powers of rulers and ensuring the liberty of citizens. Once again, however, it is elites other than the political who can exercise alternative forms of power and the leadership of intermediary organizations who exert whatever influence such groups have. In other words, this pluralist position emphasizes that the competition is not only between politicians and stresses that there is no single homogeneous political elite; but, at the same time, it accepts Schumpeter's characterization of democracy as consisting largely in the competition between elites.

The position can be criticized on two grounds. In the first place, whilst democracy is in some sense bound up with the diffusion of power, is it not necessarily to be associated with the separation of powers, that is the existence of a number of separate power centres? Responsible government might in practice be more easily maintained in a centralized power system than in one in which the determination of policy is scattered amongst different groups or agencies. Certainly the problems of establishing popular control over a multiplicity of elites are bound to be greater than those of controlling a single elite. This is really just to restate the points made in criticism of Dahl's theory of minorities rule.

Secondly, the mere fact that a number of different power centres exist, that an extensive set of checks and balances operates, is of itself no demonstration of the democratic nature of a system. The influence that General Motors may be able to exert on American government policy no more demonstrates American democracy than the barons' influence over King John demonstrated Plantagenet democracy. Even Schumpeter, with his limited requirements, saw democracy as being distinguished by an elective procedure to decide who is to hold governmental power. His successors should certainly demand no less. That a government is sensitive to the views of church leaders, industrialists, military chiefs, even trade union officials, does not make it susceptible to popular control, simply susceptible to control by church leaders, industrialists, military chiefs and trade union officials. Within such a diffused system of power, the crucial variable is whether or not the separate centres of power are themselves in any sense responsible to a wider electorate.

Much of the confusion in this debate springs from the lack of any clear classification. If any meaning is to be given to the word democracy, it must surely be distinguished from elite rule. The position of the original elitist theorists is clear; democracy can never exist. The argument of their successors, that democracy is a particular form of elite rule, is simply a confusion of language. We should be clear about the limits of this criticism. There may be much to be said in favour of rule by the knowledgeable and informed, as much to be said for a system of checks and balances and as much again for a 'mixed' polity in which the element of popular control is strictly circumscribed. There is little to be said for identifying democracy with one or other of these.

E

2. EMPIRICAL GENERALIZATIONS

Political typologies, and in particular the continuum of democracy, aristocracy and monarchy, have never been innocent of empirical reference. Theorists have used the past and their own present to find examples of their ideal types of approximations to them, to illustrate what they thought to be the workings or the consequences of each type, and to underpin generalizations about the environment in which different regimes would emerge or flourish.

With the professionalization and growth of 'political science', the amount and the quality of such information have increased and improved. We have now a good deal more knowledge, and more systematic knowledge, about political systems than was available to classical theorists. This has led to the demand that our theorizing should be different not only in quality but in kind; and nowhere has the demand been more insistent than in discussion of democracy. We should not, it is often asserted, merely be carrying on a traditional debate or exploring old concerns in the light of our more extended knowledge, but should be restructuring the nature of the discussion. We should be constructing what, it is claimed, is a novelty—an empirical theory of democracy.

What can be meant by an empirical theory of democracy? An answer has been attempted by some recent exponents of the enterprise.[6] All political theories, they say, are cast in one or more of three moulds—normative, analytic or empirical. Normative theory attempts to justify particular values and to suggest the institutions, policies or social behaviour which would instate or enhance those values. Analytic theories are concerned with conceptual analysis. Empirical theories are descriptive and explanatory, built up from observations of the real world. Traditionally theories of democracy have been normative and analytic, containing only a small and unsystematic empirical ingredient. Under the stimulus of behavioural political science, however, a new type of theory can be created. Its primary

[6] *Empirical Democratic Theory* (Chicago, 1969), edited by Charles F. Cnudde and Deane E. Neubauer, pp. 1–3.

feature, its best claims to be a specifically empirical theory, are firstly that it is non-normative and its practitioners disavow any attempt to justify values or prescribe to politicians and citizens; secondly, it is directed at 'the description and explanation of observable phenomena, as opposed to hypothesized or conjectured occurrences'; and lastly, it is scientific in going beyond the casual empiricism of traditional theory and seeking to construct causal hypotheses which can be inter-related and are capable of being tested empirically.

Some misgivings immediately present themselves. It could be objected that the first condition, normative neutrality, is either unnecessary or impossible. It is unnecessary if it is meant to imply that empirical work directed by some practical objective must lose its scientific respectability. That a researcher may wish, and may state his wish, to preserve democracy (or perhaps to improve it) no more invalidates his work scientifically than if a marine biologist confesses to a desire to remedy water pollution. More fundamentally, it may be that any theorizing about democracy must include at worst assumptions or at best analyses which are in some sense normative. It could be objected to the second condition that, if theory is directed towards observation rather than hypothesized events, this possibly excludes any theorizing properly speaking and certainly excludes one of the most apparently profitable lines of advance, economic theory. To the third condition, it could be objected that empirical theory does not in fact give rise to causal hypotheses and indeed that causal explanation is an import into rather than an export from this area.

Before these objections can be pursued further, some attempt must be made to describe the sort of generalizations about Western democracies put forward by political scientists. Broadly speaking, much of this work falls into three areas of investigation. One covers the question of the conditions necessary for the inauguration or the maintenance of a democratic system. Another is to do with the working of democratic institutions, and much effort here has been directed towards electoral and party behaviour. The last area covers investigations into the ways in which, in democracies, government outputs in terms of legislation and policies are affected by pressure from below, with the study of pressure group activity dominating. Here only some of the major works within the first area will be discussed as examples of empirical theorizing.

The conditions of democracy

Several different approaches have been explored in the search for the environmental conditions on which Western democracies depend. Some writers have looked at socio-economic factors, others at ideological or cultural factors, and others have investigated the relationship between governmental and non-governmental institutions.

Amongst those who have sought to establish the socio-economic conditions of democracy, there have been two distinct approaches, one largely historical, the other quantitative.

The historical approach has dwelt on the common features in the development of those societies which have produced democracies. Perhaps the best known and certainly the longest established thesis is that of Marx. Democracy is the outcome of bourgeois capitalist society and emerges as a product of the more or less violent overthrow of feudal forms of property ownership and of aristocratic political regimes. The position of political institutions in Marxist theory is somewhat ambiguous. On the one side, they are seen as epiphenomenal, secondary products of the economic system which adapt themselves to changes in the productive process. At the same time, control of the governmental apparatus can be used by governing classes to protect patterns of property ownership even though they are becoming increasingly anachronistic in terms of the productive system. Therefore, despite economic determinism, the revolutionary, whether bourgeois or proletarian, must aim at political objectives and the seizure of political power. The type of regime created by a new governing class will be appropriate in some way to the property system which defines and gives economic power to that class. Although Marxists have not been entirely consistent in their attitudes towards democracy, the usual argument has been that it is the regime appropriate to bourgeois capitalism. As in much orthodox liberal doctrine, a connection is established between competitive politics, trading in votes and a pluralistic social order on the one side and a market economy on the other, with the additional implication that in such a regime the control of economic power will always be the final determinant of the exercise of political power. The type of political order fully appropriate to a proletarian society will in fact be not democracy but the absence of a political regime, at least in the sense of a system of coercion.

This theory of the historical determinants of democracy, stressing as it does the inauguration of democracies in bourgeois revolts against aristocratic domination and their dependence on a capitalist economic order, faces a number of difficulties. In the first place, it is not clear that the social origins of Western democracies can be delineated in such stark terms. Secondly, it seems doubtful if capitalism is either a necessary or a sufficient condition for democracy. If industrialization is a component of capitalism, it does not seem to be a necessary condition since democracy has been both inaugurated and maintained in largely agricultural economies. Nor is capitalism plausibly a sufficient condition, since fascist regimes have emerged in advanced industrial nations. Perhaps more crucially, capitalism at least in the form of state capitalism has been produced by socialist regimes without this resulting in, or being expected by Marxists to result in, liberal democracy.

A variation on the Marxist theme attempts to take account of this last difficulty. This is the 'convergence thesis' which lays emphasis not on capitalist ownership but on industrialization as the historical determinant of democracy. Very broadly, the argument is that two major political consequences of industrialization have affected or will affect in common the political structures of all advanced industrial nations, both Communist and non-Communist. The first is the need for increased governmental intervention in order to stabilize an increasingly complex economy and to mitigate the social dislocation produced by rapid economic change. The second set of consequences creates a climate more hospitable to the growth of democratic forms. An advanced industrial system will give rise to a common culture. This culture —urban, rationalist and based on high levels of educational achievement—will encourage the spread of democratic institutions. Further, since industrialization depends on increasing division of labour and skills, it will add to the number of interest groups making demands within the political system and so encourage the social pluralism in which democracy flourishes. Lastly, the affluence created by industrialization will undermine totalitarian regimes, for a high mass consumption society cannot support the extremist fervour and revolutionary dedication such regimes require.

Other attempts to trace the socio-economic factors affecting the development of democracy put more emphasis on agriculture and patterns of land-holding. Dahl, for example, accepts the convergence thesis when looking at industrial societies, but he also points out that agrarian societies have varied in their receptiveness to democracy. Following Tocqueville, he distinguishes between traditional peasant society and a free farmer society. Peasant society is marked by cumulative inequalities in wealth, status, and the means of coercion which result in a sharp inequality of political resources; this is fertile ground for hierarchic hegemonic regimes. In contrast, in a free farmer society land distribution is more equal, norms are egalitarian and the means of coercion are dispersed; and this is a society more receptive to democracy. The crucial variables for Dahl are the degree of social pluralism and the degree of dispersion of economic, coercive and intellectual power. Just as industrial societies can vary in these respects and consequently prove more or less receptive to democracy, so too can agrarian societies. The difference is that, whereas there is a thrust towards social pluralism in advanced industrial nations, twentieth-century pre-industrial societies conform to the traditional peasant rather than to the free farmer pattern.[7]

The most strenuous recent attempt to provide an alternative socio-economic explanation to the Marxist has been that of Barrington Moore.[8] With Marx, he relates the evolution of democracy to the rise of capitalism and to a bourgeois revolution, but he argues that what is decisive for political development is the way in which this process of modernization has been carried

[7] *Polyarchy*, pp. 53–61, 71–80, 82–8.

[8] *Social Origins of Dictatorship and Democracy* (London, 1967), particularly pp. 413–32.

through. In particular, the nature of the agrarian revolution and the reactions of the rural classes to modernization have been crucial. The major variables affecting democratic development have been the relations of the landed class with the monarchy, the attitudes of that class towards commercial agriculture and its position *vis-à-vis* the urban bourgeoisie. Although in the early stages of modernization a strengthening of central monarchic authority was necessary, a decisive precondition for democracy has been the achievement of a rough balance of power between crown and aristocracy. Equally decisive has been the response of landed aristocrats to the pressure on them to expand their cash incomes. Amongst the alternatives open to them—alienating the land from the peasantry and using free labour as the means of commercial farming, trying to increase traditional exactions from the peasantry, or engaging in commercial farming through the use of forced labour upheld by political means—only the first has been favourable to democratic development. The relationship between the landed class and the urban *haute bourgeoisie* has also been crucial, for it has only been in the absence of a convergence of interests between these two classes that peasant and working-class demands for political reform have stood any chance of success. The implication of the argument is that, for democracy to emerge, the landed aristocracy has had to win both independence of the crown and a secure economic base in order to constitute a countervailing power to the urban bourgeoisie. In sum, Barrington Moore follows Tocqueville rather than Marx in stressing the importance for the growth of democracy of rural development and in isolating social pluralism rather than class hegemony as the historical basis for Western democratic regimes.

Clearly, attempts such as these to relate political to socio-economic development are not novel. Equally clearly their intuitive and discursive historical cast cannot satisfy the demands of those who would construct a new empirical theory of democracy. The root demand of these aspirants is that any hypothesis about the relationship between socio-economic factors and democracy should be quantifiable; we cannot speak of what we cannot test, and we cannot test what we cannot number. The focus of attention in consequence shifts. The concern is not with the common elements in the historical development of modern democracies, but with the socio-economic characteristics which democracies now show or which correlate with the incidence of democracy.

One of the first to turn his attention to these problems was Martin Seymour Lipset.[9] The hypothesis he set out to test was that democracy is related to the extent of economic development. This required his constructing indices of both democracy and economic development. In looking at European and English-speaking countries, Lipset distinguishes on the one side stable democracies and on the other unstable democracies and dictatorships. His requirements are less stringent when he looks to South America, for there he distinguishes between stable dictatorships and 'those countries which have not had fairly constant dictatorial rule'. As indices of economic development, he takes wealth, industrialization, education and urbanization. In every case, the average level of economic development is higher in the more democratic countries; for example, the average *per capita* income is higher in European and English-speaking stable democracies than in European and English-speaking unstable democracies and dictatorships, whilst it is higher in Latin American democracies and unstable dictatorships than in Latin American stable dictatorships. The evidence is rather less impressive when the ranges within each category are examined, for, whilst the lowest level generally falls within the less democratic and the highest level within the more democratic groups, this is not invariable and the overlap on most of the indices is very considerable. Lipset adds some explanations of these correlations. Increased income and better education induce the lower strata to accept a more gradualist and less ideological view of politics. Modernization creates a larger middle class with an emollient effect on political conflicts. It tends to create a common life style between higher and lower classes. It stimulates tolerance or at least indifference by making it less important to individual citizens who wield governmental power. Finally, it produces a complex of intermediary organizations which can act as counterweights to government and as schools of citizenship.

[9] See his article 'Some Social Requisites of Democracy' in *American Political Science Review* (March 1959) which is largely incorporated in Chapters II and II of his *Political Man* (London, 1963, paperback ed.), pp. 45–96.

Developments of this type of analysis have consisted largely in paring away some of its methodological defects. One such development has been to transform Lipset's twofold categorization of democracies and non-democracies into a continuous variable by awarding countries points according to the existence over time of an effective party system and an executive derived from an electoral process. The degree of political development (in terms of democratization) can then be correlated with indices of economic development. The initial conclusion from the utilization of this procedure has been that there is a high degree of association between political development and indices such as levels of communication, urbanization, education and employment in agriculture, with communications being most clearly associated. Further examination of the evidence has suggested that there is no simple linear relationship between socio-economic and political development, such that the more advanced a country socially and economically, the stronger the tendency for it to be 'advanced' (that is, democratic) politically. It suggests rather that there are upper and lower thresholds. Below a certain socio-economic level, the chances of democracy are negligible and variations do not affect those chances; equally, above a certain level, the propensity to democracy is strong but further raising of socio-economic level will not increase its strength.[10]

Some general conclusions can be drawn from this empirical work. There is a significant association both between the various indices of modernization and between these indices and the maintenance of stable democracy. At the same time, the relationship is neither absolute nor linear; countries at the same socio-economic level can be either democracies or non-democracies, and both below and above certain levels variations in socio-economic achievement do not seem to affect the political outcome.

A quite different approach to the problem of defining the environmental conditions in which democracy can be maintained consists in the attempt to discover its ideological basis, the par-

[10] See Phillips Cutright, 'National Political Development' in *American Sociological Review* (April 1963); Irma Adelman and Cynthia Taft Morris, *Society, Politics and Economic Development* (Baltimore, 1967); Deane E. Neubauer, 'Some Conditions of Democracy' in *American Political Science Review* (December 1967); Robert A. Dahl, *Polyarchy*, pp. 62–80.

ticular pattern or patterns of attitudes and values which (it might be postulated) must be present in either the whole population or a particular influential segment of it if a democratic polity is to be sustained. To put this another way, the enterprise is to delineate the political culture within which democracy can flourish. The most extended attempt up to now to identify the democratic political culture (or what they call the 'civic culture') has been made by Almond and Verba.[11] Their book centres on what has become, in this type of empirical investigation, the almost obligatory critique of 'classical' or 'textbook' depictions of democracy. Traditionally, participation has been stressed as the value to be maximized and the characteristic most firmly identified with democracy. However, a comparative study of the knowledge of, feelings about and judgements in political matters in the United States, Britain, Germany, Italy and Mexico reveals both that there are differences of political culture between these countries and that the culture of the two countries with the most stable democratic systems (Britain and America) do not follow the lines of this traditional template.

What are the general characteristics of the civic cultures of Britain and America? There is considerable awareness and knowledge of the impact of government on the lives of individuals and interest in political affairs. Pride in the political system, expectations that governmental officials will operate fairly and considerately, feelings that everyone is free to engage in political discussion are all comparatively widespread. Whilst there is considerable partisanship, that is emotional involvement in electoral decisions, this is not extended to intense social or personal antagonism between political groups. Acceptance of the obligation to be an active citizen is combined with a general feeling that, either individually or in concert, men are capable of influencing governmental actions. There is a considerable measure of mutual trust in interpersonal relations and a high valuation of co-operative qualities such as generosity and consideration for others. In sum, the civic culture consists of a mixture of counterbalancing attitudes of which those associated with the active citizen form only a part. It balances respect for authority and independence of it,

[11] Gabriel A. Almond and Sidney Verba, *The Civic Culture. Political Attitudes and Democracy in Five Nations* (Boston, 1965, paperback ed.).

men's acceptance of their role as subjects and their assertion of their role as citizens, involvement and apathy, partisanship and mutual trust, consensus and cleavage. These balances are achieved partly by individual inconsistencies, particularly the gap between men's actual involvement and their feelings that they can and ought to intervene politically. Partly also the proper mix is achieved by cultural differentiation between classes, for within the civic culture active attitudes are more closely associated with the more highly educated groups and passive attitudes with the less educated. This psychological and social balance of citizen competence and subject competence is, argue Almond and Verba, the appropriate cultural milieu for a democracy since it fits the contradictory demands made of a democratic government, that it should govern and that it should be responsive to its citizens.

The implications of this type of argument are exposed more fully in another line of investigation concentrating on the beliefs and feelings of political activists. Much of this investigation has arisen from an effort to test the frequent assertion that a wide consensus on values, and particularly on those involved in the democratic 'rules of the game', is necessary to a stable democracy. On the evidence, the claim has little foundation, at least if the United States is taken as an example of stable democracy. Although there is fairly wide assent in the American public to abstract statements of the democratic credo, there is little agreement—and certainly nothing that could plausibly amount to a consensus—on concrete applications of those principles. However, subscription to democratic values is greater amongst the better educated, those of higher socio-economic status and the politically active. Even in such groups, harmony is far from complete, but there is much stronger support amongst them for democratic norms such as freedom of speech, political equality and mutual trust together with a much firmer faith in the legitimacy of democratic procedures. Although there is no common view amongst the investigators on the precise relationship between shared democratic values and the stability of democracy, there seems to be some agreement that the beliefs at least of political activists have some significant effects on the chances of democracy and that within democracies it is the elite groups, who are fortunately also generally the most politically influential, who are the carriers of the democratic creed.[12] Complementing this conclusion are those studies which attempt to show that the lower classes are comparatively more authoritarian than the middle and upper.[13]

A third approach to the question of identifying the environmental conditions necessary to the maintenance of democracy has concentrated on the relationship between governmental and non-governmental institutions. Eckstein's *Theory of Stable Democracy* is one good example of the genre.[14] Eckstein initially attempts a definition of stable democracy. Essentially, it is that, to be democratic, a system must have elections deciding the competition for power and policies and, to be stable, it must have endured for a long period, not as a result of historical 'accidents' but through a capacity to make effective adaptations to change and to achieve shared political goals. Eckstein finds previous answers to the question of what are the conditions necessary to stable democracy—answers in terms of procedural consensus, an extensive non-ideological and pragmatic outlook, a co-operative party system—both obvious and uninstructive and claims that what is needed is a general theory of governmental stability. This he provides with the argument that stability depends upon patterns of authority within the governmental system being congruent with those in other social institutions. Obviously authority patterns would be congruent if they were identical, but in a democracy this is impossible since democratic relationships are unattainable or undesirable within such structures as the family, the school or the workplace. Eckstein partially avoids the apparent dilemma by weakening the claim that full congruence is needed to the claim that 'graduated resemblances' are needed. Some structures such as political parties are close to government, others such as the family are more distant. Democracy will be stable if those structures close to government

[12] See James W. Prothro and Charles M. Grigg, 'Fundamental Principles of Democracy; Bases of Agreement and Disagreement' in *Journal of Politics* (May 1960); Herbert McClosky, 'Consensus and Ideology in American Politics' in *American Political Science Review* (June 1964); Robert A. Dahl, *Polyarchy*, pp. 124–88.

[13] See S. M. Lipset, *Political Man*, pp. 97–130.

[14] The *Theory*, originally a monograph, appears as Appendix B in *Division and Cohesion in Democracy: A Study of Norway* (Princeton, 1966).

resemble it in their authority patterns. The dilemma is, however, only partially avoided, for Eckstein also implicitly accepts that, because of the necessity for authoritarian patterns in non-governmental structures, a fully democratic government would inevitably be unstable. The cure for these ills of democracy is apparently less democracy. Attaching himself frankly to the old ideal of 'mixed government', Eckstein accepts that government authority patterns cannot be entirely democratic if congruence and thus stability are to be achieved.

In providing an explanation for this claimed connection between stability and congruence, Eckstein turns to a psychological link. Strain and anomie can arise when men are subject to different and conflicting normative demands, and this is the case where incongruence of authority patterns exists. Thus there will always be a psychological impetus to remove any institutionalized differentiation of roles demanded of the individual.

In some ways, Eckstein's theory is a particular instance of a more general and ubiquitous argument connecting governmental and non-governmental institutions. This is the pluralist argument, stated in its essentials by Tocqueville but frequently extended and elaborated in recent writings.[15] In essence, the pluralist position is that a democratic system depends upon the presence of a complex of independent organizations and social groupings mediating between the individual and the state. In the absence of such intermediary institutions, in a 'mass society', dictatorial or totalitarian regimes are likely to emerge, whilst their presence is at least a necessary if not a sufficient condition for a stable democratic regime.

A variety of reasons have been presented for this connection between democracy and a pluralistic social order. In the first place, political resources are dispersed throughout the community in such a society. By coalition, men who as individuals would be powerless to affect either government or other groups can create instruments of influence. Independent and voluntary organizations can act as countervailing powers against the state and prevent the hegemony of any one social group. They constitute an essential bar to the cumulative inequalities typical

[15] The most sustained statement in recent years is in W. Kornhauser, *The Politics of Mass Society* (London, 1960).

of hierarchic societies. They disperse also political skills and aptitudes. By presenting wide opportunities to participate at a micro-level in decision-making, they stimulate both the desire and the ability to act on a wider political stage. They formulate political demands and represent these demands to the public at large, to the parties and to government direct. In doing so, they make coherent and stabilize the views and interests of groups within the population who would otherwise have no means of clarifying let alone pressing their opinions. Lastly, they serve, in many circumstances, to moderate both the attitudes of individuals and the demands of groups. The process of bargaining within groups, between groups and between groups and government provides a wide education in the spirit of compromise and co-operation essential to democracy. Besides this, the fact that many individuals are members of more than one group and these affiliations may cut across each other is likely to divert them from extreme positions. An implication of this last point is that not all patterns of pluralism and cleavage will prove hospitable to democratic institutions. Where group affiliations are cumulative, in other words where the membership of different groups falls along the same major dividing line in the community, political polarization may be too acute to support democracy. To put this another way, societies with a high level of subcultural pluralism, whether the subcultures are based on class or race or language, may find democracy difficult to sustain. At the same time, it is often argued, all the processes subsumed under the term 'modernization' lead to the kind of diversification and moderate cleavage necessary to democracy, and indeed this connection probably explains both the association between socio-economic achievement and democratization and the limitations of that association.

The explanatory value of empirical theory

We can leave here this brief sketch of the different approaches to the question of the conditions necessary for the maintenance of democracy and return to our first inquiry. How far does this sort of investigation constitute or form the basis for an empirical theory of democracy? Reflecting on this material we may have good reason for doubting at any rate any excessive claims made about its theoretical implications. Going back to the original definition of empirical theory, we can put two questions and try to answer them in the light of this survey of work on the conditions of democracy. In what sense are the empirical theories presented explanatory and productive of empirical hypotheses? In what sense is this discussion non-normative?

The limitations of the explanatory force of findings on the socio-economic or cultural conditions of democracy are partly the consequence of the limitations of statistical correlations as explanations.[16] In the first place, the investigator has to make a preceding decision on what variables to attempt to correlate with democracy. It comes as no surprise to find that socio-economic level and political culture have been chosen. It might have been surprising if average height or average mean temperature had been picked. For we will probably approach such questions with a previous expectation, derived from all sorts of assumptions about social causation, that, whereas size and hours of sunshine are irrelevant to political behaviour, economic prosperity and values or beliefs are likely to prove relevant. However, a moment's reflection might persuade us that there is no *a priori* improbability about there being a significant correlation between the variables we have rejected and the incidence of democracy. We might accept the possibility of a significant association between average height and democracy, but probably only because we could appreciate a possible association between height and socio-economic development. This assumption in itself might be sufficient to convince us that any correlation between height and democracy would be spurious and that it would be profitless to pursue this line of investigation. A further moment's reflection might show us that the variables we have rejected could also be regarded as important by others. Given Montesquieu's theory of the relationship between climate and political institutions, it would be quite plausible for a latter-day Montesquieu to correlate average temperatures with democracy. To say this is not to urge new frontiers for empirical research, merely to illustrate that our

[16] See W. G. Runciman, *Social Science and Political Theory* (Cambridge, 1965, paperback ed.), pp. 123–32.

very choice of which correlates to test implies a frame of reference, implies at least an assumption that we shall find a significant association. In this sense, statistical studies of this sort can merely confirm, or fail to confirm, previous social judgements. The symmetries we seek are, not unnaturally, those we expect to find.

A second difficulty is that even if we assume a direct causal connection between two variables that are statistically associated, we may not be able to decide the direction of the causal flow. Let us take the example of Almond and Verba's discussion of the civic culture. The conclusion they reach seems to be that a certain profile of attitudes, present in Britain and America, works in favour of stable democracy. Where, as in Germany and Italy, it is absent, democracy must be insecure. One objection to this conclusion could be that political culture (like average height) might itself be a dependent variable explicable in terms of some third factor. Another could be that, in the absence of any demonstrated temporal sequence, it is possible to route the direction of causality the other way. The most obvious differences between Britain and America on the one side and Germany and Italy on the other is that the former have had a longer and more consistent experience of democractic politics; indeed, this is presumably at least one reason why Almond and Verba characterize them as stable democracies. But it is at least as plausible that the attitudes embodied in the 'civic culture' are a product of this stability and continuity as that they are a cause of them. Alternatively, it is possible that some countries are objectively less democratic than others and this explains variations in attitudes. For instance, the fact that fewer in Germany and Italy than in Britain and the United States see themselves as capable of influencing national government could possibly be due to a greater sensitivity of British and American governments to popular pressures and electoral opinions. The attitude may, in other words, be an accurate assessment of a political reality. This certainly also seems a plausible interpretation of the correlation between education and the sense of civic competence; the less educated (who are also in all likelihood the poorer) may *feel* less able to influence government because they *are* less able. Certainly, the evidence presented does not of itself invalidate the argument of such 'classical' theorists as Tocqueville and John Stuart Mill that democratic attitudes would grow with experience of democratic procedures. Indeed the argument is implicitly supported by Almond and Verba, for when they try to account for differences in national cultural profiles they resort to the peculiarities of particular national political histories as an explanation.

This points to the widest lacuna in this kind of statistical analysis. In deciding what correlations to test, when the correlations have to stop and which is the direction of causality, we usually have some rough theory of social causation in mind. Alternatively, once a statistically significant association has been established, the task of explanation has only just begun. This is recognized, at least implicitly, by some of the writers who have been mentioned. Lipset, after establishing the connection between economic development and democracy, explains it in terms of the effects of modernization on attitudes, the class structure, the pattern of group interests and the growth of social pluralism. These explanations are in no way derivative from the statistical analysis itself. In the same way, assuming (what is far from the case) that Eckstein has established a correlation between 'congruence' or the existence of 'graduated resemblances' and government stability he too has to offer explanations in psychological terms in no way derivable from the correlation itself.

In sum, the explanatory value of this type of quantitative analysis is strictly limited and it is not productive of causal hypotheses which can be tested empirically. It is a way of testing causal hypotheses usually derived from general and intuitive historical reflection; or it establishes connections which have then to be explained. In this sense it is not a theory of democracy at all, if the point of a theory is to produce hypotheses about causal connections in the real world. As we shall see, it is less heuristically productive than economic theories of democracy; and it departs from traditional theory only in that it seeks to establish its empirical generalizations in a much more rigorous and systematic way. This, of course, is in itself a considerable gain.

F

The normative content of empirical theory

The other claim put forward by empirical theorists, that empirical theory is non-normative, has in recent years given rise to a great deal of heated and, it shall be argued here, largely justified criticism. Much of the criticism denies the freedom from value assumptions often asserted as the hallmark of political science and its derivative empirical theory. In conducting this attack, the critics often accept the same notion of a 'normative' theory as those they criticize, a theory which justifies or recommends a particular set of values or institutions. On this definition, a non-normative theory would be one in which no partisan stance is taken up by the theorist. However, in another sense of the term, no empirical work on democracy can escape being 'normative' since it cannot avoid the need for a definition of democracy based on a statement of democratic ends. Whether or not we approve of these democratic norms is, in this context, irrelevant. Simply to isolate those systems we are to distinguish as democratic or to place systems on a continuum according to their degree of 'democraticness', we have to have in mind some notions of what democracy means, some (to refer back) ideal type of democracy. Now it might be argued that any definition of democracy can and should itself be drawn from empirical investigation. To return to the Founding Father, this seems to be Schumpeter's position. Classical definitions of democracy are faulty since they picture conditions entirely absent in the real world; therefore a new definition is needed which will fit the actual characteristics of real world democracies. But how are we to decide what are to count as real world democracies? Even if everyone agreed on the list, this would presumably imply they had a common definition in mind as well as a common assessment of real world systems. But there is little comfort in appealing to a consensus of opinion, for ascriptive disagreements do in fact exist. Such disagreements can only be resolved by reference to some stipulated definition of democracy which must precede and cannot flow from empirical inquiry; and there are linguistic boundaries to such stipulated definitions. Schumpeter, as we have seen, steps beyond them.

The need for a precise normative definition of democracy

increases rather than decreases with the sophistication of the empirical inquiry. An investigator like Lipset who wishes to distinguish broadly between categories of democracy and non-democracy in order to test socio-economic correlates can afford a rough and ready definition (say, any system like the American and British). To go beyond this and to establish democracy as a continuous variable which can be correlated with, for instance, indices of modernization requires both a more precise definition and one, such as Dahl's, which is posed in normative or maxi-mizing terms. Moreover, differences in definition at this stage might have important effects on the findings. If, for example, we define democracy in terms of competition between elites and popular election of rulers and use indices of democracy derived from this definition, we might get different correlations than if we define democracy in terms of political equality and produce indices based on this definition.

Thus, no matter how morally indifferent or politically neutral an investigator might be, he is bound to attempt a normative definition of democracy and he will then be making choices which can affect the nature of his results. In terms of the categories of theory put forward at the beginning of this section, this would no doubt count as analytic theory for empirical theorists. But, once the necessity for analytic theory as a precondition of empirical work has been admitted, it is difficult to see the importance of normative neutrality. To say that a writer chose political equality as his definition of democracy rather than electoral competition between elites because he approved of political equality is to say nothing that would invalidate whatever findings he may produce. Moreover, supposing it to be desirable, such moral neutrality may not be possible. For the line between defining a system in normative terms and approving or disapproving of it is a thin one. Even if it is one worth defending, it is doubtful if we have to hand a language aseptic enough to keep tones of commitment entirely out of our discourse.

However, the major charge against empirical democratic theory made by critics is a much broader and more damaging one. It is that, far from being non-normative and distinguishable from classical theory on this count, it does covertly press a particular ideological position, and is distinguishable from classical theory in having abandoned some central democratic values. To some degree, the debate has been both simplified and distorted by too rigid a definition of battle lines. On the one side, empirical theorists often start from a caricature of 'classical' or 'textbook' theories of democracy: the fact is that there is not a great deal in common between say Rousseau, Bentham, Tocqueville and John Stuart Mill (who would presumably figure in any list of classical theorists) and certainly they do not share those features often imputed to 'classical' theory. On the other side, critics incline to the same vice, lumping together all recent writers on democracy and ignoring the methodological and possibly also ideological gulfs that divide them.

What, however, are the precise charges brought against empirical or revisionist theory?[17] The hardest pressed is that, whilst it is explanatory in form and is initially aimed at the elucidation of the workings of existing democratic systems, it does by implication if not overtly defend an elitist view and reject a value central to traditional theory, popular participation in politics. Behind this *trahison des clercs* (in the view of the critics) lies a loss of faith in the mass of men as capable of exercising any proper judgement in political matters. The basic assumption is that most men are incapable of understanding the complexity of governmental decisions, of adhering with any steadiness to liberal humane values, or even of sustaining with any enthusiasm democratic procedures. Fear of the people and in consequence a desire to restrict their entry into the political process has replaced the older liberal faith in the innate virtue of the common man. This fear originates in a reaction to totalitarian movements and regimes which, unlike older authoritarian structures, have sought to mobilize mass support as a means both to achieve power and to

[17] See E. E. Schattschneider, *The Semisovereign People* (New York, 1960); T. B. Bottomore, *Elites and Society* (London, 1964); Peter Bachrach, *The Theory of Democratic Elitism* (London, 1969); Carole Pateman, *Participation and Democratic Theory* (Cambridge, 1970); Graeme Duncan and Steven Lukes, 'The New Democracy' in *Political Studies* (1963); Lane Davis, 'The Cost of Realism: Contemporary Restatements of Democracy' in *Western Political Quarterly* (1964); Christian Bay, 'Politics and Pseudopolitics' in *American Political Science Review* (1965); Jack L. Walker, 'A Critique of the Elitist Theory of Democracy' in *American Political Science Review* (1966).

retain it. The fear has been fortified by a considerable body of evidence showing the extent of political ignorance, apathy and authoritarianism even in established democracies. The older liberal enemies—despotic kings, arrogant aristocracies, exploitative plutocracies—have consequently been replaced by a new enemy, the people or the masses themselves. Their instincts and attitudes, their apolitical apathy and ignorance, make of them poor material for their traditional role as carriers of the democratic and liberal creed. Indeed, any deep incursion by them into politics, any rapid mobilization of their numerical strength, is likely to be a harbinger of authoritarian trends rather than a hallmark of stable democracy. Liberal democracy does depend, and must depend, rather on a commitment to democratic values amongst the elites. It can survive a lack of agreement on democratic norms amongst the people at large, but it requires at least a relative consensus amongst the politically active and effective. Stable democracy exists where there is such consensus and where crucial decisions are largely confined to these elites. The democratic element lies in the lack of homogeneity between elites, their mutual competition and the minimal popular participation involved in choosing a master.

This new stance, according to radical critics, involves more than a simple redefinition of democracy on empirical grounds; it implies a set of normative judgements which fly in the face of values traditionally associated with democracy. In particular, it rejects what have been thought to be essential objectives, political equality and individual participation in communal affairs. For, in traditional theory, popular participation is not merely a contingent definitional characteristic of democracy dispensable under a more 'realistic' redefinition. To further the development of men as men by lifting them to a political dimension is the very object of democracy, what makes the system valuable. The point of democratic procedures is not (or not just) to ensure good governmental decisions, but to widen individual experience. To accept as proper a limitation of that experience on the grounds that this makes for better governmental decisions is to miss this point and to alter and debase the normative terms of the argument. At bottom, to the critics, attempts to revise democratic theory sacrifice this central participatory ideal for the sake of values such as stability and equilibrium, values which dominate not only American political science but American sociological theory generally. It is this concern with the stability of present Western democracies rather than any scientific imperative that has determined the thrust of empirical research.

These criticisms, harsh as they are, are just. It needs no sensitive nose for a value judgement to smell out the political commitments of revisionist or empirical theories, and the values implicit in them certainly depart from those supported in some traditional theories. Not that the revisionist normative position is entirely without precedent. Although few modern revisionists have recognized their ancestry, it follows a long tradition stretching back to Polybius for which mixed government has been the ideal. To a large extent, the so-called redefinition of democracy has been an exercise not in science but in semantics. On older meanings of the term, what Schumpeter and his successors are saying is that democracy, undiluted, is either a bad or an impossible regime. Other values such as stability, efficiency or tolerance must be secured by institutional safeguards. The old language of 'mixed government' recognized this multiplicity of ends and the diversity of forms necessary to achieve them. The modern mode has usually been more evasive. Instead of saying that democracy should be limited in the interests of other ends which cannot be achieved or might be harmed by democratic procedures, it has bowed to the popularity of the term and insisted that democracy *means* mixed government. The redefinition becomes a means of escaping the unwelcome charge of being undemocratic. And it is made the more acceptable since, describing a balance which (it is asserted) exists, it can lay claim to some sort of scientific status.

Defending a situation that does exist is, of course, not necessarily more exact, scholarly or scientific an enterprise than urging one that does not exist. Knowledge of the real world might certainly influence our ambitions. Investigations showing how narrow are the social or economic or ideological bases on which democracy rests might make us more cautious in our hopes for establishing democracy. Those showing that existing democracies, although not fully realizing democratic ideals, nevertheless do satisfy other legitimate ends might dilute our enthusiasm for change. All the same, such investigations cannot refute democratic ideals. Or they cannot refute them unless it could be demonstrated that in no conceivable circumstances can such ideals be fully realized, or more fully realized than at present; and, even if such a demonstration lies within the compass of empirical investigation, we are far from reaching it.

Nevertheless, it could be said in answer to radical critics that, although they are right in pointing to the normative assumptions of empirical theorists, they are too hasty in rejecting those norms. Equally desirable political ends can after all conflict, and it might be important for even the most ardent and radical of democrats to know the circumstances in which democratic procedures can successfully be introduced or if an extension of popular participation will risk the disruption of even the limited democracies (in participatory terms) which we have at present. Stability, at any rate of regimes which are justifiable on other (including democratic) grounds, is surely a good; and some sacrifice of further democracy might be justified if it assures the possession of that which we have.

To weigh this apology we must look at the way in which a concern with stability has affected empirical inquiry and the degree to which the connection often asserted between stability and certain features of present liberal democracies has actually been established.

The concern with stability can in the first place shape the kind of question which is asked and can thus determine the focus of empirical research. Lipset, for example, takes as the starting point of his investigation into the socio-economic and ideological bases of stable democracy the question, under what conditions can a society have 'sufficient' participation to maintain the democratic system without introducing sources of cleavage which will undermine the cohesion?[18] Consequently, when he comes to framing the categories which he correlates with socio-economic level, they are determined not so much by how democratic a system is as by how stable it is. Now the question asked could have been otherwise. Could not Lipset have asked, and asked no less 'scientifically', whether or not there is a relationship between

---

[18] *Political Man*, pp. 32–3.

increased levels of participation and greater instability or, if there is such a relationship but it is neither absolute nor linear, under what conditions a society can increase levels of participation without introducing those sources of cleavage promoting lack of cohesion. No doubt such inquiries would probably be prompted by a different concern, with participation rather than with stability. Yet such research would be no less scientific, no less empirical, no less realistic.

The first relationship, that between increased levels of participation and instability, is assumed or at any rate only very sketchily argued in much of the literature. Two pieces of evidence are usually brought up in support—firstly the fact that periods of intense and extended political activity, such as in Germany in the early thirties, have coincided with the growth of totalitarian movements, and secondly the findings that the apolitical and the apathetic, those who presumably would be brought into the arena by further participation, have little attachment to democratic norms and are attracted by authoritarian and Manichean ideologies normally the prerogative of extremists movements. Neither of these pieces of evidence provides support for the view that greater participation would produce greater instability.

Two unspoken assumptions inform much of the discussion on the conditions of stable democracy, that democratic systems will stabilize only at a single level (which is accepted as otherwise desirable) and, in consequence, that no system could be stable at a greater level of democracy than is achieved in present stable democracies. The moral attractions of stability as an end in itself are limited. Its desirability depends very much on whether or not the situation stabilized is itself desirable. It is not surprising that those of a conservative cast of mind have avoided this moral problem by presupposing that whatever is, over a long period, is right and that social or political systems have an inbuilt tendency to revert to a desirable equilibrium position. The notion of a Providential 'natural harmony', so often harnessed to conservative thinking, has survived even in modern areligious social science. Pre-Keynesian economists could not accept that a situation of mass unemployment was stable; there was then no need or no possibility of political action to remedy it. Similarly, Parsonian sociologists represent society as a homeostatic system, a functional whole with a capacity for self-adjustment which will bring it back to some central position of equilibrium; and, at least in systems such as the American, it has been assumed that this still, calm centre is desirable—or, at any rate, that it would be as irrational to reject it as to reject the motions of the stars.

Some such assumptions inform discussion of the conditions of stable democracy in two ways. In the first place, 'stability' is granted a different status than any other social end, and consequently inquiries into the prerequisities of stability are given a different status than inquiries into the prerequisities of any other social end. Since stabilization is assumed to be intrinsic in the social or political system, since the stability of a particular system is assumed to be dependent on self-adjustment rather than on deliberate action, research into the prerequisites of stability is research into what is intrinsic in the political mechanism, different in kind and more scientific in its purchase than inquiry into, say, the prerequisites of increased participation. For questions about the realization of goods which can be achieved only by deliberate choice take on a Utopian hue, whilst questions about those ends supposedly realized independently by the system take on a superior scientific hue.

The other outcome of the functionalist stance is a covert assumption that whatever can be isolated as the common characteristics of present stable democracies are necessary features of any democratic system that is to be stable. Since in present stable democracies the ordinary man is only marginally involved in political activity and competitive elites largely engross political life, any further extension of popular participation is likely to create instability. In the main, the lesson taught is that more democracy means less secure democracy.

It is a conclusion by no means entirely consistent with the evidence brought forward in its favour. Let us look again at Eckstein's argument. Stability, he claims, requires some congruence or resemblance between the authority patterns in government and in other social institutions. Now it is certainly plausible that problems might arise if there is no such correspondence, not necessarily because of the anomie arising from conflicting normative demands on the individual, but simply because people might seek to apply norms found to be satisfactory in one sphere to other spheres. Eckstein draws the conclusion that, as authority structures in the family, the school and the workplace cannot be democratic, the governmental structure cannot be wholly democratic either. Even if the premisses of the congruence argument are accepted, this conclusion hardly follows. It could well be the case for instance that, if men are used to a democratic political system, they might start demanding some democratic procedures or controls in the workplace. If (as Eckstein assumes) these demands could not possibly be met, one could only conclude that stable democracy is impossible since such men would hardly be satisfied with less democracy in government as a means of reintroducing congruence. Congruence might be necessary to stability since men may not differentiate between different authority structures and may ask for the establishment of what they regard as a satisfactory pattern in all of them; stability would not result from the imposition of a pattern generally regarded as unsatisfactory in all of them. If Eckstein is wrong in his assumption that change is impossible or undesirable in the family, school or workplace, the alternative conclusion from his premisses would be that democracy in the big political battalions requires democracy in the small social platoons, a conclusion that would not have surprised a Tocqueville or a Mill.

Another example of the same defects of argument can be found in Almond and Verba. Again their criticism of activist theories, stressing the role of an active citizenry in the maintenance of democracy, is not altogether supported by the evidence they offer. At the most general level, their findings show that acceptance of an obligation to participate and feelings of competence to participate are more widespread in Britain and the United States, the stable democracies, than elsewhere. This would seem to buttress the traditional case. However, Almond and Verba go on to argue that the civic cultures of Britain and the United States diverge from the activist model in two ways. In the first place even those who feel most capable of acting politically maintain a respect for authority which modifies the intensity of their intervention; and secondly, whilst there are many who are active in politics, there are also many who are content with the passive role of subject. It seems to be accepted as a conclusion by the authors that radical departure from this particular balance would weaken democratic government, and in particular that any further approximation to the activist model would prove unsettling.

Quite other conclusions would be compatible with their findings. The first ground for objecting to the activist model cannot bear much weight. Despite national differences, a relationship exists between citizen competence and subject competence; in other words, those who feel they can influence government are most likely to be persuaded of the general fairness and competence of government officials. This is by no means incompatible with the activist model; it has often been supposed that participation would be connected with feelings of satisfaction with government, if only because active citizens might have some capacity to ensure government actually satisfactory to themselves. Nor does it follow from this relationship that further participation would produce instability; rather the reverse.

The second objection to the activist model is really the crux of the argument. The ideal of participatory democracy is flawed because stable democracy requires different attitudes in different groups of the population, some having an appreciation of their role as citizens, others displaying a decent deference to authority. The political cultures of the two stable democracies, although they conform more closely than the others to the activist model, are mixed in this sense. The sense of competence as a citizen is unevenly distributed. More specifically, different educational groups (and therefore, one can infer, different socio-economic groups) differ in their political confidence. Again, however, it does not follow that a disturbance of this balance through greater participation amongst the present non-participants would necessarily produce instability. And again the reverse argument is at least as plausible. In general terms, two syndromes emerge from the findings. At least within Britain and America, those who see themselves as active citizens are also more likely to be politically informed, politically engaged, satisfied with their political role and the performance of government, committed to democratic values, proud of the political system, trustful in their relations with others and active in voluntary social organizations; on the other hand, those who are alienated as actors from the political system tend to show the opposite cluster of characteristics. Given that actual participation increases the sense of political competence and that satisfaction with the performance and general legitimacy of the regime makes for stability, it would seem to follow that greater participation would enhance rather than detract from the stability of democratic regimes. Equally, it would seem, restriction of the scope of participation might give rise to alienated groups who stand as a potential threat to democracy.

It is plain at this point that the major difference between participatory or traditional theorists and elitist or revisionist theorists is not so much empirical as terminological. The disagreement stems from the different meanings attached to the term 'participation'. For the revisionist, the fact that the mass of men are ignorant, apathetic, alienated and liable to be seduced by anti-democratic movements is standing proof that anything more than their marginal participation is dangerous to democracy itself. To many traditional theorists, the same fact would indicate the urgent need to extend participation, both because this is the object of democracy and because it is only through participation that ignorance, apathy and alienation can be overcome. As Tocqueville urged, it is never a good argument against giving a group power that it is irresponsible in its attitudes, since it can never learn to be responsible if it is excluded. It seems clear that what are involved here are different notions of participation. Perhaps rightly, the revisionists fear the sudden mobilization of those whose attachment to democratic values is tenuous and conversely welcome the apathy of those whose interest could only be menacing to democratic procedures. But there is a wide difference between the sudden mobilization of previously disengaged groups and the kind of regular involvement in communal affairs that has been the aim of classical participatory theorists. What such theorists wanted was the extension of popular involvement through what might be called constitutional participation. The symbols and instruments of democratic advance were for them the township meeting, the parish council, voluntary associations, workshop democracy. In contrast, it often seems, the symbols of increased participation for revisionists are the mass rally and the street demonstration. Clearly, there is a world of difference between constitutional participation and this type of mass participation. Equally clearly, we are far from a position where we can disprove the assumption that further constitutional participation is compatible with stable government and indeed is likely to reduce the dangers of a 'mass society'. In consequence, we are far from a position where we can discredit the ideal of participation by associating it inextricably with instability.

The degree to which such an ideal is realistic depends on the extent to which the conditions necessary to it are susceptible to alteration by political, that is to say deliberate, action. If further diffusion of participation is dependent on greater material equality or improved popular education, any realization of this democratic ideal will be dependent on the malleability of the distributions of material or educational resources. Looked at another way, the ideal is realizable to the degree that political institutions can at least contribute to the creation of the conditions necessary to their own success. It was a crucial if generally implicit assumption of much classical theory that political decisions, particularly decisions about the constitutional framework, were important for democratic development. It is by no means clear that this is mistaken. For instance, if the existence of democratic institutions helps to create those attitudes in turn supportive of democracy, if the legal protection of voluntary associations and so of social pluralism is more likely in a democratic than a non-democratic society, then the hope that democracy is in some self-sustaining may not be entirely vain.

A common feature of the sociological approach to politics is its neglect of this possibility, and it is perhaps in this blind spot that its ideological bias is revealed most distinctly. Politics are generally seen as epiphenomenal, a merely secondary product of deeper social, economic or cultural factors. In consequence, political institutions are treated almost invariably as dependent variables not acting upon but acted on by their social environment. This is not merely a methodological deficiency, for it implies if it does not conceal a particular political bias. It affects heavily our view of how extensive is the effective range of political action, and thus the pessimism or optimism with which we estimate the possibility of consciously achieved change. The desire to remove discussion of democracy from political theory and to make it part of sociological theory is at least in one of its aspects the outcome of a passive rather than an active mood. For traditionally political theory has talked of what is subject to human will (if only through self-restraint), whilst sociology has traditionally talked of those conditions too deep or too complex to be within the scope of conscious manipulation. Political theory, in one of its most persistent pursuits, has pointed out desirable changes in society. Sociology has had the function of saying why things are as they are; it has sometimes slipped into the role of telling us why they can be no other.

3. DEDUCTIVE MODELS

An economic theory of democracy

A third mode of discussing democracy lies in the construction of deductive models. It is often termed 'economic', and here we shall refer to the economic theory of democracy. The adjective is appropriate in a number of ways. In the first place, the structure of economic theories of democracy is similar to the structure of economic theory in general. Such theory starts, not from broad propositions about the social or the political system as much of contemporary sociology does, but rather from propositions about individual behaviour, axioms of individual psychology. It sets the goals assumed to dictate individual action within the theory; it stipulates the invariant elements of the environment in which individuals act; and it deduces either their behaviour given changes in the variable elements of the environment or the reactions of one person or set of persons to changes in the behaviour of others. In this way, it attempts to produce, by way of deductive reasoning, hypotheses about relationships and behaviour in the real world. Obviously enough, such hypotheses will have validity only to the extent that men do in fact act as the behavioural axioms postulate and the real world environment does approximate to the conditions stipulated in the model.

A second justification for labelling these theories of democracy economic is that they share with economic theory a common and narrow definition of the goals to which individual action is directed. Just as in economic theory firms act to maximize profits and consumers to maximize their own utility, so in the economic theory of democracy parties act to maximize votes and voters to maximize their own utility. Like *homo economicus, homo politicus* is a rational consumer paying for policies he wants with his vote; and the political like the economic entrepreneur seeks either to provide what the market wants or to manipulate the market. This points to another common assumption of the theories, which is that men act rationally. By this is meant that, whatever particular goals an actor might have, he seeks to act efficiently, to maximize benefits to himself and to minimize costs to himself.

A third reason for calling such theories of democracy economic is that they have been developed originally by professional economists and have emerged as a product of certain problems of welfare economics. The difficulties that welfare economists have had in defining and settling rules for measuring a general social welfare function have led some such as Arrow to seek a solution to the problem of determining social choice on the basis of individual valuations by translating it into a constitutional problem, a problem of choosing the social decision procedure. The problem of defining social welfare is thus transformed into the problem of isolating the ways in which constitutions which allow for the political expression of individual preferences (by voting) may achieve a summation of individual values.

These are the only ways in which the adjective 'economic' can appropriately be applied. The theories are not economic in the sense that they imply any economic causation of political phenomena. They do not attempt to explain why political structures are as they are, which is precisely what a theory of economic causation such as Marxism purports to explain. Moreover, so far as they do, in stipulating motives for action, suppose democratic politicians to be acting solely for their own 'political' reasons (maximizing votes) and not in any sense to sustain particular class interests (unless such support proves to be politically profitable), they rest on contrary assumptions to Marxist explanations. These theories are not 'economic' in the sense that they presuppose that men act on economic motives, unless 'economic' here is identified with self-interest. The self-interest axiom is basic to these theories, and it may be that the limitations of this axiom set some limits to the applicability of the theories, but it is not essential to them that interest be narrowly defined in terms of possession or exploitation of economic resources.

The application of this method to political problems has given rise to a considerable literature in recent years. Here, the discussion will be based on the work most directly concerned with democratic theory, Anthony Downs's *An Economic Theory of Democracy*. As basic axioms, Downs postulates an electorate of rational voters and politicians whose aim either immediately or in the long run is the winning of elections. For the voter, the point of voting is to affect government policies in such a way as to benefit himself; for political parties (which Downs treats as homogeneous bodies), all actions are intended to maximize votes and policy decisions are merely means towards this end. He stipulates also the characteristics of democratic government: there are periodic elections in which all sane, adult permanent residents cast one vote and through which one party (or coalition of parties) out of a number is given the powers of government until the next election; governments do not restrict the political activities of citizens who are not committed to their violent over-throw, nor do losing parties use illegal means to deprive the victors of the fruits of victory.

On the basis of these two sets of assumptions—on individual behaviour and on the institutional environment—he constructs a basic logic of voting and of government decision-making. The voter's main concern is to assess which party will benefit him most in the period of office after the election. Downs assumes that in establishing these party differentials the voter cannot rely on electoral promises (an assumption that is neither self-evident nor necessarily required by the theory); the voter will therefore compare the benefits, the utility income, he has received from the incumbent government with those he thinks he would have received if the alternative parties had been in office. In a two-party system he will vote for the party he consequently most prefers; in a multi-party system this might be modified if his favoured party has no chance of winning. Governments will spend in such a way as to gain most votes and finance that spending in such a way as to lose fewest votes. The position is complicated by the need of governments to watch the competitive moves of the other parties. In this political warfare, the party in government stands at a disadvantage. Its best strategy is to follow the wishes of the majority on each issue, for otherwise the opposition can stand on the same ground on every issue (except those in which the government is supporting a minority) and thus win. However, if it does follow this strategy it leaves open the possibility of its competitor supporting intense minorities and so building up a majority coalition of minority dissenters.

Downs introduces into the basic logic the effects of uncertainty, the absence of sure knowledge about the course of events, and the related effects of the costs involved in gathering information. The major effect of uncertainty on government decision-making is to enhance the political influence of intermediaries between voters and rulers, such as interest groups, which can inform government about what the people want. Uncertainty about the effects of individual policies on his interests makes it rational for the voter to rely on the ideologies of parties as guides to their choice. Information costs, when weighed against the small part which each vote plays in deciding elections, are so great that the rational voter would not pay the price of being generally informed on politics. However, in areas where he has already specialist information, and his own interests are heavily involved, additional information costs will be small, the benefits to be gained from changes may be large and the citizen will intervene. The rational citizen is an indifferent voter but an active lobbyist.

Economic theory as a recommendatory theory

In this way, Downs believes it possible to construct a number of propositions, capable of being tested empirically, about the behaviour of governments, parties, voters and citizens within a democratic system. The logic behind some of Downs's propositions might be queried, but this would perhaps be no more than to acknowledge that his was a pioneering work. What is more to the point here is to look at the general structure of this kind of theory and to examine its capabilities. Two questions in particular will be examined. Firstly, how far is this type of theory recommendatory and how far is it explanatory? Secondly, what are its possibilities as an explanatory theory?

G

The distinction being used here between recommendatory and explanatory theory is simply that the first ends with or includes injunctions about how men should act or what sort of institutional frame they should construct or maintain, the second aims solely at detailing the mechanisms governing their actual interactions. Downs makes a somewhat different distinction; his theory is, he claims, neither normative nor purely descriptive but positive. A normative theory would start from certain goals and sketch the behaviour needed to achieve those goals, that behaviour then being translated into a set of ethical injunctions. His economic theory is not normative in that the conditions stipulated in the model 'merely describe what is done in society'. Neither is it descriptive, since it excludes all but economically rational behaviour and stipulates only some of the many variables that might affect the real-world political situation. It is positive in the sense that it explains what will happen given certain conditions, which may or may not wholly correspond to reality.[19] There are difficulties in this distinction of Downs. It is by no means clear what a 'descriptive model' would look like. More importantly, it is not clear whether or not he sees a 'normative' theory as necessarily differing radically in structure from a 'positive' theory. It will be argued here that 'positive' theory in Downs's sense can be either recommendatory or explanatory.

It might seem superfluous to insist that economic theory can be recommendatory, given the propensity of economists to offer advice to governments, businessmen and consumers. Surely, it might be argued, the very commitment to constructing models of rational behaviour implicitly involves the theorist in recommendation. In the present context, it might be said that, since the theory indicates what the rational man *qua* voter or politician will do, and since it is presumably always better to act rationally than irrationally, then an account of the logic of voting and of government decision-making is an account of how men should act. The economists' answer to this charge is that rationality is a function of means not ends. The ends themselves are non-rational and towards them the theorist can remain in the academically hallowed state of ethical neutrality. The goals a decision-maker

---

[19] Anthony Downs, op. cit., pp. 31–4.

does pursue or wishes to achieve are, for this type of theory, data from which the theorist must start in his analysis of the best means of attaining them, that is the means involving the least expenditure of scarce resources. The element of recommendation involved narrows down to the norm that, whatever a man's ends may be, he should act in the most efficient way to reach them.

Nevertheless it is doubtful if the economic theorist is so divorced from decisions about ends. The very nature of this type of theory might require his specifying *some* goals of individual behaviour and it might also require his excluding certain sorts of goal. It is, in the first place, impossible to identify rational behaviour without specifying fairly precisely the goals to which it should be directed. It cannot be claimed that an economic theory can take into account the whole universe of ends which individuals may pose for themselves. No model of rational behaviour could be constructed without some narrower specification of the goals which are to be considered appropriate in the model, for rationality is specific to a particular end and action which is rational in relation to one end may be irrational in relation to another. The point is illustrated well by one of Downs's examples of irrationality. A man prefers party A to party B on grounds of its probable performance in government, but he votes for party B since otherwise his wife might throw a tantrum. The action is perfectly rational in relation to the end given priority by the actor; he does presumably achieve domestic harmony. In order to define the act as irrational, it is necessary to discriminate between the actor's possible goals. The 'political function of elections', Downs says, 'is to select a government. Therefore rational behaviour in connection with elections is behaviour oriented towards this end and no other.' It is not that this procedure is in any way illegitimate. One can readily see that, without some such restriction, no model building would be possible. The point is simply that, in order to detail the logic of voting or of government decision-making, the theorist cannot be concerned solely with the deduction of means; he must, if he is to construct a model at all, select from all the possible ends actors might have for behaving in a certain way that which is to form the standard for rational action in the model.

There is a further difficulty. It might be thought that, given the assumption that voters act to select a government, an economic theory can take into account any ends they may pose which will determine their preferences between parties. This is not so, or rather there are some an economic theory cannot incorporate without serious loss of analytic rigour. Barry has pointed this out in his illuminating comparison of what he labels as the 'sociological' and 'economic' theories of democracy.[20] Any wants can be fitted into an economic frame provided a sufficiently liberal definition of utility maximization is accepted, but the cost of such liberality is the bankruptcy of this type of theory. More specifically, the theory cannot incorporate any altruistic goals to which individuals may hold, goals that may lead them to base their political preferences on some general social value or on an assessment of benefits and costs to others. To say this is not necessarily to charge economists with having a worm's-eye view of human nature or of committing themselves to ignoble values. It is merely to say that the theory can operate effectively only within a limited range of human wants.

The definition of rational behaviour, which is after all the objective of an economic theory, is then dependent on the specification of ends and on the assumption that self-interest, narrowly defined, is the goal of individual action. Nevertheless it could still be said that the depiction of rational behaviour is not a recommendation to act in this way, unless of course the theorist is addressing an audience of self-interested actors with the same ends in mind as those posed by the model; in which case, the value choices are those of the actors and not of the theorist. From this standpoint, the fact that such a theory can be constructed only for a limited set of human goals does not constitute a commendation of those goals, just a possible limitation of the explanatory force of the theory.

Let us then consider another possibility, not that an economic theory is necessarily recommendatory, but that it can be either recommendatory or explanatory depending on the political stance and perhaps also the historical position of the theorist. How far, if at all, does the structure of a 'positive' theory (to use Downs's phrase) determine whether it is recommendatory or explanatory?

[20] Brian M. Barry, *Sociologists, Economists and Democracy* (London, 1970, paperback ed.), pp. 14–16, 31.

To answer this question, it would be useful to go back in time and examine the Benthamite theory of democracy.

Although Downs does not recognize his intellectual forebears, indeed seems to see Rousseau as the only classical theorist who has written on democracy, the Benthamite discussion of democracy closely resembles modern economic theories. Nor perhaps is this surprising, since the utilitarians were as influential in developing the dismal science as they were in the development of political theory and carried over some assumptions and methods from one to the other. What briefly are the elements of Bentham's democratic theory? He put it forward as a psychological axiom that men seek their own interest, defined by him as the pursuit of pleasure and the avoidance of pain. He believed also that the proper end of government action as of moral rules was the achievement of general utility, defined as the greatest happiness of the greatest number. In some areas, notably in most aspects of economic behaviour, men's pursuit of their own interests leads automatically through the market mechanism to the general utility. In other areas, the protection of private property for example, government needs to intervene in order to promote the general utility. It can do so by imposing legal penalties on behaviour threatening social utility or by bestowing rewards on behaviour enhancing it, and these penalties and rewards can be calculated sufficiently accurately to ensure that individual utilities will always be better satisfied by acting for the general good than against it. In his early life, Bentham believed the self-evident truth of these ideals would be enough to recommend them to British rulers. When later he learnt the imperviousness of rulers even to self-evident truths, he turned to the constitutional problem, how to ensure that rulers themselves would follow the general interest. He saw now that how rulers decide is a determinant of what they decide, and that merely to discover what governments should do is no guarantee of their doing it. The attitude he consequently took, more in keeping perhaps with the psychological postulates of his utilitarian theory, was that rulers will inevitably follow their own interests as individuals. The political problem was therefore to discover the constitutional conditions under which it would be in the interests of governors to follow the general interest. The answer, at least in Britain, was the construction of a democratic system in which rulers could only maintain themselves in power by attending to the wants of the people and individual voters could further by their votes only those interests they shared in common with all other members of the community. The complex of institutions he recommended—universal suffrage, the secret ballot, annual parliaments and so on—was intended to achieve these objectives.

Many flaws may be found in this argument, some to do with the acceptance of the utility principle as self-evident, others with the belief that it can be aggregated from individual utilities. One crucial ambiguity lies in whether the democratic method is seen as a calculus by means of which the greatest happiness of the greatest number can be computed out of different individual utilities, or whether Bentham saw each separate voter as voting with the general interest in mind (even though from self-interested rather than altruistic motives). If the second is what Bentham was arguing, this would clearly separate utilitarian theory from economic theory. Clearly too utilitarian theory is recommendatory and had no 'descriptive' value at all, since no democratic system of the Benthamite type existed in Bentham's time. Despite these differences the Benthamite model shares a structure of argument with the economic theory. The strategies do not coincide. Bentham, assuming the self-interested voter and politician, tries to define the institutional requirements necessary to ensure that governments will act in certain desirable ways. Putting forward much the same psychological postulates and assuming certain characteristics of a democratic system roughly equivalent to Bentham's requirements, Downs tries to deduce the behavioural consequences. Bentham asks what institutional frame is necessary to produce a given pattern of behaviour; Downs asks what patterns of behaviour will follow from a given institutional frame. The same structure of argument can be turned to alternative purposes.

The Benthamite example suggests that an economic theory of democracy need not be tied purely to an explanatory purpose. How far is Downs's particular theory purely explanatory? To explore this, we might look at his complaint about the previous treatment by economists of government behaviour. They have, he argues, supposed the proper social function of government to be the maximization of social welfare and have supposed further that governments will in fact perform this function once economists have provided them with the knowledge of how to do so. In consequence, the efforts of economists have been directed (unsuccessfully) towards defining what social welfare is. They have, in short, ignored what economic thinking assumes axiomatically in looking at all other social agencies apart from governments, and all other persons apart from rulers, that the discharge of social functions is a by-product of men's pursuit of private ends. With Bentham in mind, there is an air of *déjà vu* about this complaint. Downs realizes, like Bentham in mid-career, that the self-interest axiom must be applied to governments as much as to private economic agents. Like Bentham again, Downs argues that the goals of rulers will vary with the constitutional frame. In the main, this is for him the basis of a plea for different theories to explain government actions in different constitutional systems. At the same time, it is clear that he believes that a democratic system such as the one he stipulates in his model is a satisfactory mechanism for maximizing social welfare, at least in the sense that it forces governments to respond to the wants of all its citizens. Since the conditions he stipulates are in his view descriptive of systems such as the American, governments such as the American are justified because they do satisfactorily discharge this social function. Thus the theory is commendatory if not recommendatory.

It would need only a change in starting point to inquire how far conditions other than the 'descriptive characteristics' Downs lists would guarantee more assuredly the apparently desired end, that is responsiveness of governments to all wants. For instance, 'one man, one vote' is stipulated, but equal opportunity to utilize political opportunities is not. Yet the lack of the second might be just as great a barrier to governmental responsiveness to all wants as the absence of the first. Nevertheless, it is worth emphasizing the values implicit in Downs's argument, because again it shows that a professed concern with what is does not exclude evaluation. Putting it at its most general, an economic theory of democracy (or of any other political system) can be recommendatory in either a conservative or a radical direction. A conservative theory, taking characteristics of existing systems as stipulations of the model, might show what desirable functions governments do discharge. A radical theory, stipulating conditions which are not present in existing systems, might show how government might better discharge those functions seen as desirable.

The general argument has been that this theoretical structure can be harnessed to explanatory or recommendatory purposes. It should be noticed, however, that it has severe limitations as a basis for recommendation since it can only serve those who see the proper end of government as the satisfaction of the actual wants of private individuals. It is relevant in a strict sense only to *homo economicus*, and would be of little help to those who saw the ends of government action or of a political system as other than the satisfaction of actual wants. If, instead of asking the question, 'What form of government will ensure that men's wants are best served?', I asked for instance, 'What form of government will best develop individuals capable of leading the good life?', this type of theory would be of no assistance (unless, of course, the good life is defined in terms of actual want-satisfaction); and this, not because the second question is any more 'normative' or less 'positive' than the first, but because this type of theory is limited in its applicability.

Economic theory as an explanatory theory

The second question that was posed earlier was what are the explanatory possibilities of the economic theory of democracy. Certainly, the theory promises a greater rigour of argument than is usual in discussions of democracy, or indeed of most other political subjects. More importantly, it offers a *theory* of political behaviour in a sense that no other mode of discussion does. Empirical generalizations about democracy generally either start from intuitive guesses about causal relationships or offer functional explanations at such a high level of generality that they give very little guidance to those with the modest ambition of understanding what causes specific events. An economic theory promises some logical theoretical grounding to hypotheses about causal relationships which may be of help in explaining particular acts and events in the real world. This, of course, is the crux of the matter for, unless complex deductive models are regarded as things of beauty and thus ends in themselves, they are justified only in so far as they do help in our understanding of real situations.

What criticisms might be made of economic theory as an aid to explaining the workings of democratic systems? The first is that it is excessively abstract. The complaint was made long ago by Macaulay in his attack upon James Mill's *Essay on Government*. 'We have here an elaborate treatise on Government, from which, but for two or three passing allusions, it would not appear that the author was aware that any governments actually existed among men. Certain propensities of human nature are assumed; and from these premises the whole science of politics is synthetically deduced!'[21] The burden of this often repeated complaint is that a deductive model can seldom comprehend all the variables affecting real-world situations and so conclusions drawn from such a model will seldom be valid in actuality. The charge is true but, it will be argued, this does not destroy the utility of such models. Certainly it is true that an economic theory is a simplification; this indeed is its point. Of course, for such a theory to have any explanatory force, the conditions stipulated in the model must approximate roughly to the characteristics of some real systems, but the correspondence can and only need be approximate. Downs's conditions of a democratic system, although he claims them as characteristics descriptive of actual systems, are not in fact wholly present in any real system and are not by any means wholly descriptive of any real system. Clearly the costs of constructing a theory descriptive of any actual system, in the sense that it stipulated all the conditions affecting behaviour within it, would probably be much too high. It would involve an inordinate increase in the complexity of the theory and a decrease in the range of its applicability. It would, moreover, require knowledge of what are all of the variables operative within the real-world situation. This would present formidable practical difficulties but it also raises the question of what the explanatory force of the theory would then be. For knowing what are the

[21] *The Miscellaneous Writings and Speeches of Lord Macaulay* (London, 1905), p. 161.

variables affecting a situation is surely a major part of our understanding of it.

Downs himself is clear about the object of the exercise. It is the production of empirically testable propositions on the behaviour of parties and voters in a democratic system and he ends his book with a list of twenty-five such propositions.[22] Some are distinctly unpromising, either because they seem to be mere restatements of the premises of the theory ('Party members . . . formulate policies as means to holding office rather than seeking office in order to carry out preconceived policies') or because they are too loosely framed to be empirically falsifiable ('Political parties tend to carry out as many of their promises as they can whenever they are elected'). But some are both genuine deductions from the basic hypotheses and are precise enough for at any rate rough empirical testing. Take, for instance, the proposition that, after a drastic electoral defeat, a party will change its ideology to resemble that of the victor. At least one obvious example to the contrary springs to mind. The most drastic defeat in twentieth-century British history was that of the Labour Party in 1931, but it would be difficult to argue that it was followed by a Labour swing to the right. Must we then either find some flaw in Downs's logic or scrap that part of the theory altogether? These would seem to be the options open if the point of the theory is simply to produce hypotheses for testing. But if it is seen rather as an aid to explanation, it can be of help whether or not the predicted behaviour occurs in the real world. If the predicted behaviour does occur, the model suggests the causal mechanism by which this result was produced (without discounting the possibility that it could have resulted from some different pattern of causation). If the predicted behaviour does not occur, the model still gives some guidance in analysis of the real-world situation since at the least it points to the probability that some variable or variables exogenous to the model affected that situation. Some *ceteris paribus* proviso must be built into deductive models, and consequently conclusions derived from them will not necessarily be valid in a generally more complex world; but this does not inevitably destroy the usefulness of such models.

A second criticism that might be made of economic theory as

[22] Anthony Downs, op. cit., pp. 295–300.

an aid to explanation is in some ways a special instance of the first; it is that the psychological postulates of the theory, that parties act to maximize votes and voters to maximize benefits to themselves, are too narrow to explain many aspects of political behaviour in a democracy. Again the charge is correct, without being as damaging as might be supposed. The theory cannot explain some very important aspects of political behaviour and cannot in principle be adapted to explain them. Let us take one obvious fact about behaviour in democracies—the fact that people do take the trouble of voting. Why do they? As Barry has pointed out, Downs's answer to this question is unsatisfactory.[23] Downs does in fact give reasons for viewing abstention as economically rational. In deciding whether or not to vote, the citizen must first determine how much difference it will make to him if one party rather than another wins (his party differential). Secondly he must calculate the probability of his vote deciding the election. If voting involved no costs, any preference for one party would make it rational to vote and only the indifferent would abstain. In fact voting does involve time costs—the costs of gathering information, going to the polling-booth and so on, and, so slight is the likelihood of any single vote affecting the result of the election, the smallest cost would deter the rational man from voting. Downs tries to explain the fact that many do nonetheless vote by bringing in the long-run benefits they derive from the maintenance of democracy. As the system would collapse if there were massive abstentions, the rational voter will incur voting costs in order to keep democracy, from which he benefits, in being. The conclusion does not hold, for the rational voter in Downsian terms would have to calculate the probability of his own vote affecting the maintenance or breakdown of the system; and, so slight is the likelihood of his vote making any difference, the rational voter would still not incur the costs of voting. The language of insurance Downs uses here is inappropriate, for the individual's receipt of benefits is not dependent on *his* paying the premium, nor is his paying the premium a guarantee of his receiving benefits.

Thus Downs's economic theory cannot provide an explanation of such a basic form of behaviour in democracies as voting. To

[23] See ibid., pp. 260–7; Brian M. Barry, op. cit., pp. 13–23.

find explanations for why people vote, we would have to move outside anything that could be assumed within an economic theory without making it vacuous. People might vote because they are irrational in economic terms, that is they have interest maximization in mind but are not adept at carrying out even the simple cost-benefit analysis which the rational voter must perform. But if behaviour is thus irrational, the model is inapplicable; or at the least, if behaviour is persistently irrational in this way, the model loses any predictive and explanatory capacity. Or people might vote because they are rational but not in economic terms. That is to say, the means (voting) are appropriate to the ends they hold, but these ends are not those assumed in economic theory. They may believe voting is a demonstration of citizenship or that they have a duty to engage in political activity, even of this minimal sort. They may alternatively feel voting for a particular party to be a symbolic demonstration of their attachment to some general political principles. They might even vote out of sheer habit. None of these motives could be reconciled with the kind of cost-benefit analysis on which economic theory depends. It could, of course, be argued that the individual acting on such motives was gaining psychic satisfactions; but, if the psychic satisfactions of altruistic behaviour are to be counted as benefits, it is difficult to see what deductive rigour could remain in a cost-benefit analysis. However, whilst the criticism that the initial behavioural axioms are too narrow to explain some aspects of political behaviour is justified, it would be wrong to exaggerate the damage inflicted by the charge. Although economic theory may be unable to provide explanations for some aspects of behaviour, it might nevertheless explain others. It may not be able to explain why people vote at all; it might nevertheless provide plausible explanations of why they vote as they do. Moreover, even if it is unable to explain why people vote, an examination of the economic argument at least allows us to narrow the range of possible explanations.

A third criticism that might be made is that economic theory can operate only within a narrow range of explanation. It can in its own terms explain how political parties adapt to changes in wants within a given population; it can to some degree explain how those wants can be manipulated by parties. What it cannot do, or can do only inadequately, is to show how particular patterns of wants arise in a community and how patterns of wants change. Downs acknowledges that whatever factors alter the distribution of political positions amongst the electorate are crucial determinants of a democratic nation's political life, but only two factors affecting their distribution are incorporated into his theory, manipulation by politicians of the ideological dispositions of the electorate and extension of the franchise. Clearly, as Downs admits, although these might be important, there are other factors which can alter and have altered the distribution of voters along an ideological scale. To take only one instance, changes in the class composition of an existing electorate might be as important as the enfranchisement of new classes in bringing about such a shift in distribution. The methodological individualism inherent in economic theory cannot provide explanations of such large-scale changes. This is understandable. The strength of the theory lies in its assumption that wants are given. It can suggest what the effects of a given distribution are and what the effects of a given change in the distribution will be. But it must necessarily leave untouched the question of how a particular pattern of wants has arisen and how and why it changes. Economic theory can tell us perhaps why and how parties shift in response to electoral demands, what party strategies are likely to be in given electoral circumstances. It cannot tell us why men want what they do want, why those wants coagulate into socially coherent patterns, and how those wants, those definitions of interest and aspiration, change over time. This is a recognizable limitation of this type of theory, perhaps more serious and limiting in the study of politics than in economics, since political wants are perhaps less coherent and rigid than economic wants, the definition of political interests more ideologically malleable than the definition of economic interests.

Explanations of elections

To explore this limitation further, let us compare the different ways in which the empirical generalizers (the psephologists) and the deductive theorists (the economists) have sought to explain elections; and thus discover the relative strengths of the two approaches.

What is the general picture of the electoral process that has emerged from empirical studies of voting behaviour? The first feature is an apparent confirmation of Schumpeter's judgement. Voters are largely ill-informed, not only about politics in general, but more specifically about issues at stake in the election campaign. Their views about what is happening during a campaign are likely to be determined far more by their previous political attitudes than by accurate information. Voters generally are not personally involved in political questions and have a very low political motivation. They are generally irrational, that is to say their decisions *qua* voters are not carefully considered as are their decisions *qua* consumers or businessmen.

Nevertheless, although the voter is generally uninformed, uninvolved and irrational, there is a coherent and consistent ordering of voting behaviour. For large numbers of voters, the vote reflects a persistent partisan position which is determined by or at the least correlates with elements in the individual's environment. Class, religion, family background, ethnic grouping, sex (considered in terms of social experience), local or regional characteristics, organizational affiliations—all these and other environmental factors go to shape the attitudes and party attachments of individuals and groups. Long-term, secular changes in these attachments are due to changes in the social environment. On the individual level, switches from one party to another or from party affiliation to abstention may follow from changes in personal circumstances, for instance from social mobility upwards or downwards. On a group level, alterations in the distribution of political opinion in the community will follow from large-scale demographic or social movements.

Clearly, such explanations of voting behaviour can be of little help in explaining why particular elections are won and lost. For it is unlikely that the swings between parties from one election to the next can be satisfactorily understood in terms of either random changes in individual circumstances or large-scale demographic movements. Generally, the psephologists have accounted for these swings by pointing out that elections are usually decided by

marginal shifts and these shifts occur largely amongst the group of
floating voters who have in exaggerated form all the characteristics (or defects) of voters in general; they are in other words even
more politically ignorant, uninterested and irrational than the
total set of voters. By the same token, the most interested and
informed are likely to be the most partisan and therefore the least
likely to determine the election result. Lest we be too gloomy
about this picture, it is pointed out, in echo of the Duke of
Wellington's defence of the unreformed House of Commons, that
the system works well. Whilst individuals are irrational, the system itself is rational. The general tendency of this type of analysis
is to emphasize the relative unimportance of campaigns, issues
and party disputes as decisive factors in the democratic process.
Long-term, stable political attachments are explicable in terms of
broad sociological factors; the short-term shifts which decide
elections take place amongst those most impervious to political
debate.

How far are these two different accounts of elections, that of
economic theory and that of psephology, compatible with one
another? There seem to be stark contradictions. One approach
postulates the rational voter, the other presents a picture of the
irrational voter; one presupposes an exact and direct interaction
between party policies and electoral responses, the other stresses
the irrelevance of the party battle to voting decisions. Some of
these contradictions are more apparent than real. Take the question of the rationality of the voter. One well-known voting
study concludes with what seems a flat denial of the postulates
on which economic theory is based: '... the usual analogy
between the voting "decision" and the more or less carefully calculated decisions of consumers or businessmen or courts ... may
be quite incorrect. For many voters political preferences may be
better considered as analogous to cultural tastes ... Both seem to
be matters of sentiment and disposition rather than "reasoned
preferences".'[24] Yet in fact these conclusions can readily be
harmonized with economic theory, if not with any plausible
aesthetic theory. If we take into account information costs, the
Downsian rational voter would be irrational on this argument.

[24] Bernard R. Berelson, Paul F. Lazarsfeld and William N. McPhee.
Voting (Chicago, 1966, paperback ed.), pp. 310–11.

For the economically rational voter will try to cut down the costs of his voting decision, and one way to do this will be to rely on his appreciation of the broad goals and achievements of the parties rather than assessing in detail their policy proposals. The economically rational voter is no more committed to a detailed study and evaluation of party proposals than is the rational consumer to a detailed chemical or nutritional evaluation of a threepenny bar of chocolate.

Nevertheless, some points of difference are real enough. In particular, as against the sociological devaluation of the importance of the political contest, the economic theory does assert and depend upon some complementarity between party strategies and voting decisions. It does assume that the politician will shape his policies to the demands of the political market; and it assumes also that the voter will decide between parties on the basis of some assessment of possible returns to himself. The theory requires the twin suppositions that parties determine their political positions by reference to expected electoral reactions and that voters will react to changes in party positions. Crudely, the sociological approach treats the party battle as largely irrelevant to the electoral decision, the economic treats it as central.

Here, there are reasons for believing the economic approach may be more fruitful. In the first place, some recent research has suggested that the previously common characterization of the floating voter is distorted, and that the vote-switcher is both more common than has previously been supposed and is not especially distinguished by his ignorance and alienation from the political system.[25] The second advantage of the economic approach, and this is no negligible gain, is its allowance for explanations far closer to the ordinary assumptions of politicians and commentators about the electoral process. On the whole, politicians, political journalists and political historians have few doubts about the matter. Democratic politicians certainly do try to formulate and expound policies attractive to voters or to dress policies decided on some other grounds in a garb attractive to voters. They do spend a good deal of time attacking their opponents'

[25] See R. J. Benewick, A. H. Birch. J. G. Blumler and Alison Ewbank. 'The Floating Voter and the Liberal View of Representation' in *Political Studies* (June 1969).

governmental record or defending their own. Journalists and commentators do try to account for shifts in electoral support, as evidenced in opinion polls or by-elections or general elections, by the popularity or unpopularity of the government's and to a lesser extent the opposition's policies. Political historians do not differ, except perhaps in coherence and hindsight. To take a random example, A. J. P. Taylor says of the 1935 general election: 'rearmament and foreign policy were pushed into the background once the election campaign started. The electors showed little interest in these questions... Housing, unemployment and the special areas were still the dominant themes.'[26] Such an assessment of the election in terms of the political debate of the time has an obvious plausibility. Of course, politicians, journalists and historians may be wrong in believing that the party battle is relevant to electoral decisions and elections constitute verdicts on the performances of governments and oppositions. But clearly we should be chary of dismissing a mode of explanation which seems to be, to so many, so satisfactory; and it is a notable achievement of the economic approach to accommodate in a sophisticated form common-sense interpretations of the electoral process.

The psephologists and the economists offer different conceptions of elections. They differ in their weaknesses. Broadly, the economists exclude the social differences and conflicts which produce political issues, the psephologists exclude the issues themselves. Their strengths are different too. The economists can trace the ebb and flow of political events within a democracy since they assume individuals acting differentially according to their views of the impact of those events on their own interests. They have put 'politics' back into the study of elections by re-emphasizing the importance of individual reactions and decisions. Sociologists, on the other hand, can trace those deeply rooted identifications and loyalties by which men place themselves within the community and give meaning to their actions within it. They can trace too the formation and distribution of those values which may be essential to the maintenance of a viable democratic system. To put the contrast another way, the economic model can give us insight into how self-interested voters (or parties) might

[26] *English History 1914–1945* (Oxford, 1965), p. 383.

H

react in different circumstances, whilst the sociologists can give us insight into how social groups identify themselves and distinguish or interpret their own 'interests' and wants.

The explanatory strengths of the two types of discussion are then different. It may not be too uncomfortable a fence-sitting posture to suggest that they are also complementary. One example of such a division of labour has already been suggested. Whilst economic theory can analyse consequences of given distributions of political position amongst an electorate, it is incapable of exploring fully the reasons for a given distribution or the reasons for changes in it; this is likely to be the province of sociological analysis, particularly if cast in an historical mould. It may be that in the particular area of electoral behaviour we have been examining, the two different types of analysis could be equally useful. Might we not think of voting decisions in terms of both long-term, secular attachments and short-term, cyclical variations? Secular attachments would be explicable in terms of a social environment and experience which is generally stable or varies only slowly for the individual as for groups. Cyclical variations in voting behaviour might then be explained in economic terms, that is in terms of individual or group responses to particular, idiosyncratic political circumstances. Whatever the possibilities of such combinations, it does not at any rate seem necessary to attach oneself in partisan fashion to one or other of the camps. Even if the two modes of analysis are not complementary they do not seem necessarily incompatible.

4. UTOPIAN SCHEMES

It is perhaps clear by now that the introduction of a fourth category, utopian theory, is in some ways unnecessary. Utopian theory may be defined as seeking to delineate a desirable state of affairs, and such an endeavour might well utilize all the modes of discussion which have been discussed in this chapter.

What might be the structure of a utopian theory? It needs, in the first instance, a definition of the ends to be achieved, a conceptual exploration of the implications of those ends and a statement of the institutional conditions logically necessary to them.

It needs some assessment of how those institutions might work in practice. It requires an examination of what exists to see how far and in what ways the real world departs from the desired state. Finally, it needs to investigate the means by which the present situation could be moved towards the ideal.

Thinking of a democratic utopia, it is obvious that the modes of discussion we have already examined could all be pressed into service at one or other stage. The definition of ends and the conditions necessary to achieve them is the work of an 'ideal type' or 'maximizing' theory. An economic theory could, in some contexts, be of use in suggesting how men might behave in a hypothetical institutional environment. Empirical investigations would be needed to measure the distance between reality and aspiration; and it might also help, if there exist societies at different levels of achievement in terms of the desired end, to establish by comparison the conditions favourable to its achievement and so possibly point towards paths of reform.[27]

We can of course construct utopias of the present as well as utopias of the future. If, for example, we discover that the gap between the ideal and the actual is very narrow, or that it is practically impossible to bridge it, the utopian strategy might end with an apologia for what exists. In this sense, much recent empirical theorizing is no less utopian in its import than classical theories aiming explicitly at change.[28]

Utopian theory, directed explicitly at political recommendation, does not then necessarily inhabit a completely different world of discourse from other sorts of democratic theory. Nevertheless, the brevity of this statement of a utopian method obscures the very considerable difficulties involved in using it as a basis for recommendation. The defining principle of democracy, it has been argued, is political equality. To maximize or to move further towards democracy is then to maximize or to move towards political equality. But there may be limiting factors restricting

[27] For an excellent attempt to utilize empirical investigation in this way see Dennis F. Thompson, *The Democratic Citizen* (Cambridge, 1970).

[28] See Ralf Dahrendorf, 'Out of Utopia', in *American Journal of Sociology* (1958), reprinted in *Essays in the Theory of Society* (London, 1968) for an examination of the conservative utopianism implicit in much sociological theory.

the extent to which we can or might want to extend equality. These may derive partly from present circumstances or institutions difficult if not impossible to change; they may derive from values other than political equality which we may wish to realize within or through the political system; or they may derive from a combination of the two. To repeat an obvious example, the size of the political unit may be a restraint on democratization. It may be in consequence that brute fact will have to temper democratic ambition; for it may be difficult or impossible to reduce the size of the political unit and, if (as some classical theorists have thought) full democracy is achievable only in a face-to-face society, full democracy is incompatible with a modern industrial state. Moreover, if bigness has its own advantages, we might be unwilling, even if we were able, to sacrifice these advantages for the sake of further democracy. Let us suppose a variegated cultural life or high industrial production is possible only within a relatively large community. We might be willing to follow Rousseau in disavowing such benefits, but we might rather wish to pursue the no doubt less heroic course of seeking to have the best of as many worlds as we can.

The intractability of the present and the multiplicity of values might then give us pause in our pursuit of political equality. The difficulties in deciding on appropriate institutions do not however end there. For the problem may not be simply to reconcile our desire for democracy with reality and with other ends to which we hold. Disagreements on what are appropriate institutions may also arise from differing views on what is to be expected, what is to be hoped for, from a democracy.

Four

THE ENDS OF DEMOCRACY

To say that political equality is the defining principle of democracy is not to imply that it is necessarily an end-in-itself, a first-order principle unjustifiable in terms of any other value. The establishment of such a hierarchy of values is seldom the way of political argument, and it certainly has not been the way in discussion of democracy. The advantages of democracy have been posed in a variety of guises. For some, democracy ensures that governments follow the general interest, for others it is a safeguard of individual liberty, for others it allows for self-government, for others again it moulds a particular and desirable cast of character. The degree of equality we demand may be determined by which, or how many, of those hopes and expectations we have in mind. And the kind of institutions which we feel to be appropriate will be similarly determined.

The question then is what sorts of ends might be achieved within a democratic system and what sort of institutional frame might be necessary to those ends posed as possible achievements.

1. THE GENERAL INTEREST

How governments act is affected by the constitutional system through which they emerge. This has been one basic assumption in much democratic theory. Another has been that democracies will ensure that governments pursue policies in the general interest or for the common good. The common character of such defences is that they see the benefits of democracy as lying in the quality of government it assures. Its strength is that it guarantees, at least more than other systems, good policies.

The rule of the few will produce government in the interests of the few, the rule of the many will produce government in the general interest. Whoever holds power will use it for their own interest, so the only situation in which the interests of all will be attended to will be one in which rulers are forced to follow the wishes of the whole community.[1] This crude claim, central to the Utilitarian theory, has been one of the most persistent defences of democracy. It is nevertheless open to a number of serious, even disabling, criticisms.

In the first place, it identifies a person's or a group's interests with the satisfaction of his or their actual wants, and this identification may not be justifiable.[2] It is easy to see why nevertheless it has been made. Any separation of interests and wants allows for an objective judgement of what a person's or a group's interests are. If such a judgement is possible, it weakens the case that all whose interests are to be taken into account must have a voice in decisions on policy. For the possibility of an objective judgement implies the possibility and even desirability of an expert judge. In consequence, those democratic theorists who have argued in general interest terms have tended either to identify interests with wants or alternatively (and more plausibly) to assert that, if the two are separable, the individual is nonetheless the best although perhaps not an infallible judge of his own interests.

Accepting one or other of these alternatives, it is still difficult to see in what sense a democratic procedure, through which self-interested citizens control government, can produce policies in the general interest. One of the Benthamite arguments depended

---

[1] The argument is put at its baldest in James Mill's *Essay on Government* (ed. Ernest Barker, Cambridge, 1937), p. 13.

[2] For criticisms of such an identification see John Plamenatz, 'Interests' in *Political Studies* (1954); Brian Barry, *Political Argument* (London, 1965), pp. 175–86.

on a definition of the general interest which confined it to those policies bringing benefits to all members of the community. The case, as put by Bentham himself, was this. Anyone possessing influence over public policy can further his self-interest in three different ways. He can use his influence for a personal gain unconnected with the benefits he derives from the enactment of the policy. In the case of the voter he can sell his vote; but bribery can be made ineffective by a secret ballot. He can pursue a sectional interest; but this possibility can be eliminated by including all sections in the electorate. Or lastly he can seek those policies which benefit all citizens including himself. It is this last interest which the democratic voter will necessarily seek to further, argued Bentham.[3] Plainly, the flaw in this argument is its unquestioned assumption that those interests an individual may share in common with all other members of the community will outweigh any personal or sectional interest in his calculation of his own net interests. It is possible that some policies could be said to benefit all. Let us suppose that the prevention of inflation or the maintenance of peace would bring some benefit to all and that there is agreement in the policies which would secure these objectives. It is still not the case that the rational self-interested voter will prefer those policies, for even if they bring some benefit to him they may not be to his net benefit. For particular individuals or groups the benefits to be gained from inflation or war might outweigh the benefits to be gained from price stability or peace; equally, the disadvantages arising from policies designed to cure inflation or maintain peace might outweigh the disadvantages of inflation or war.

Another Benthamite argument was that the democratic procedure, rather than being a method of expressing common interests, was a method by which the general utility could be computed out of different individual utilities. Every individual would vote in accordance with his individual interests, but, somehow, this would produce results working for the greatest happiness of the greatest number. Macaulay was only one of many immediately to point out the fallacy. The democratic procedure might produce government in the interests of the majority but

[3] J. Bentham, *Plan of Parliamentary Reform, in the Form of a Catechism* (revised ed., 1818), pp. 15–30.

this was by no means equivalent to government following the general utility. In particular, a poor majority, in pursuit of its own interests, would seek an egalitarian redistribution of property, a course which all Benthamites agreed would be a disaster on utilitarian standards. Benthamites, answering such charges, were forced to the argument that a self-interested poor majority would not disrupt the property system. One support for this claim was to repeat the obviously insecure argument that the maintenance of property was a common interest since property laws protected the poor in their possessions as much as the rich in theirs. Another was that, even if the poor would benefit in the short run by redistribution, they would lose in the long run because of the general decline in prosperity. So, provided the poor majority was rational (and state education would see to that), they would respect the existing property system. Again this argument is insecure since it is by no means necessarily true that a decline in general prosperity (assuming this follows from equalization) will bring outweighing disavantages to those advantaged by redistribution.

This argument is not of purely antiquarian interest; it is still used for instance to back the unlikely proposition that it is against a group's interests to be granted a large wage increase. However, the general difficulties in the Utilitarian argument have led to its modification into a much less vulnerable position, that democratic procedures are likely to secure governments sensitive to the wants of a population. They ensure that all wants are taken into account and that government will try to satisfy as many wants as possible. On the majoritarian argument they will always try to satisfy the wants of the greatest number; on Dahl's 'rule by minorities' argument, the wants of intense minorities will be satisfied. Either way, democratic government is that which will be most concerned to achieve the highest aggregate of want-satisfaction.

Clearly, this defence has considerable force. Even if individuals are not necessarily the best judges of their own interests, they are usually the best or most consistent advocates of their own wishes. And the threat of electoral defeat wonderfully concentrates the mind of elected rulers on the wishes of the electorate or those sections of it who are politically crucial. Of course, other types of government cannot entirely ignore popular wishes, and democratic governments may override them on the grounds that there is a divergence between wants and some general good. It is likely though that non-elective regimes will prove less sensitive to popular wants than elected governments. Equally, there are pressures on responsible governments to prove their case for ignoring popular wishes within the relatively short time-span between elections.

In its presently most familiar form, the argument that representative democracy is an adequate mechanism for aggregating wants takes on a group character. Bentham's hope that the individual voter will cast his ballot with only those interests in mind which he shares with all others in the community has generally been abandoned. The more common assumption is rather that the individual will cast his vote on some calculation of his net interest. Although purely personal interests (say, where bribery or intimidation is possible) and general interests may enter into this calculation, those interests which he shares with more limited groups (sectional interests in Bentham's terminology) are likely to dominate. In any interest calculation, a man's role as trade-unionist, property-owner, Catholic or black is likely to be of a greater significance than his role as a member of the whole community deriving common benefits from governmental policies. Within the group interpretation of democracy, this fact is not only accepted but applauded. Representative democracy encourages the formulation and representation of group demands and it also makes governments responsive to those demands. As we have seen, Dahl's theory of 'rule by minorities' suggests the mechanisms through which these ends are achieved—the electoral sensitivity of parties to intense minorities and the everyday activity of pressure groups.

A complementary definition of the general interest has been put forward. On this view, only very rarely can a policy be in the general interest—in that it is a shared concern of all members of the community. Only that (presumably fairly empty) class of policies supported by a complete consensus of opinion would be in the general interest. Given this difficulty, the only meaningful definition of the general interest is when applied to those policies which take into account the differing interests affected by a governmental decision and achieve a mutually satisfactory compromise between them.[4] In this sense, representative democracy does promote the general interest since it allows the expression of all sectional interests and encourages government to seek a compromise between them.

Some criticisms of this view have already been put in relation to Dahl's theory of 'the rule of minorities'. It assumes that all groups have equal access to the resources necessary to undertake effective action and it assumes that groups will act only to influence those policies affecting them in some way more acutely than the majority. These assumptions may not be, probably are not, true; and in consequence the cover provided by group activity is less comprehensive than the theory suggests. The root mistake is the supposition that needs can be equated with effective demands. If a democratic polity is analogous to a free market, it is as true of the political as of the economic market that only those with the ability to pay can translate needs into effective demands. And the distribution of political resources may be as uneven as the distribution of economic resources. If we are to take seriously the view that the point of democracy is primarily to secure the adequate representation and reconciliation of group wants, we should probably have to think in terms of reform rather than self-congratulation. We would have to identify the under-represented groups and to think of ways in which their weight in the political bargaining process could be increased. We might look to state assistance in the formation and maintenance of the interests of say consumers or the poor. The state has, after all, for long taken on the responsibility for organizing geographical representation. We might look for ways of widening access to the mass media. We might seek to regulate pressure group organization to ensure greater internal democracy within groups or greater public knowledge of details of their membership or finances. The point is, however, not to sketch a blueprint for a group utopia, merely to show that this theory of democracy no more excludes the possibility and perhaps the desirability of reform than other, apparently more radical, theories.

What is generally left unclear in this kind of analysis is the precise relationship between group activity and political democ-

[4] See, for example, J. D. B. Miller, *The Nature of Politics* (London, 1962), pp. 52–65.

racy. Specifically, is a democratic structure necessary to the effective representation of group demands? So far as group demands are taken into account by governments because of the fear of electoral reactions, the connection between democracy and group representation is apparent. But, at least in relation to organized groups, the connection is less apparent or at any rate direct. It could be said of very few organized groups that their strength, *vis-à-vis* government, lies in their power to direct their members' votes towards one party or another. That power is much more likely to spring from sources other than any ability markedly to influence voting behaviour. Trade unions and business associations are likely to be attended to by governments more because of their industrial than because of their electoral power. Apart from any threats (aside from electoral threats) that groups may be able to mount against government, governments may desire the co-operation of organized groups as a means of informing and even executing their own decisions. In other words, it is quite possible that governments even in non-democratic systems might have motives for deferring to the wishes and seeking the co-operation of organized groups. The strongest connection between organized pluralism and political democracy is probably the need, common to both, for a wide freedom of association. To the degree that democracy is likely to sustain freedom of association, to that degree are organized groups a feature of this type of political regime. By the same token, if democratic regimes restricted freedom of association and other regimes allowed it, the power of organized groups would be neither assured by the existence nor denied by the absence of democracy.

The most telling criticism of this defence of democracy in terms of its representation and reconciliation of group interests is that it is based on a one-sided if not false view of the political process and of the role of government. On this model, democracy is akin to the free market in which all groups bargain for favourable policies and governments, acting necessarily as arbiters, decide the terms of the final settlement. Apart from the facts that entry into the market is restricted, bargaining powers are unequal and their existence may not depend on the existence of representative democracy, the analogy rests on an inadequate view of the political process since it assumes that all social conflicts are reconcilable and that goverments are neutral in their attitudes towards these conflicts. Neither assumption is necessarily true.

A very noticeable gap in this type of analysis is its virtual disregard of power and coercion as elements in the settlement of political conflicts. It assumes some harmony of social interests; or to put this another way, it assumes that all political conflicts are non-zero-sum conflicts, in other words conflicts in which there is some possible settlement giving benefits to all protagonists and in which benefits to some are not offset by losses to others. This is the settlement which, on this view, is in the general interest, and it is one which democratic governments will have every motive to achieve. There are a number of reasons for thinking this view at the least only partial. In the first place, at the risk of repetition, groups do not have equal resources of power either in relation to each other or in relation to government; they can in some instances enforce a settlement either independently or through utilizing government powers. In these cases, even if there is a possibility of a non-zero-sum settlement, it may not be the settlement conceded by the participants with most power. However, secondly, not all conflicts are reconcilable. In the economic area, where the bargaining model is most appropriate, many might be. In other areas, the possibility is more remote. Take, for instance, conflicts between racial groups over civil or political rights. It is difficult to see the shape of a non-zero-sum settlement here; compromise might be reached, but only on the basis of concessions on one side, concessions which may be likely only as a result of some threat on the other. In such situations, governments will generally have willy-nilly to commit themselves to one side or another, rather than acting as neutral arbiters. This brings up the third and last objection, that governments are not necessarily neutral towards group conflicts. They may have their own ideological biases or (less pejoratively) principles. Or they may incline towards those groups capable of inflicting some damage on them. Either way, governmental intervention in intergroup conflict might not consist simply in deciding what the equilibrium of forces is; it might rather be a way of bringing governmental power to the support of particular groups and particular interests.

Again the limits of these criticisms should be recognized. The defence of democracy in terms of want-satisfaction is no debased ideal. It is at least a defensible scale of priorities that places the removal of unhappiness, the satisfaction of palpable felt wants, in the order above real or imagined deficiencies in the human condition which are unreflected in actual feelings. To say this is not to imply that Western democracies have in any way reached a perfect representation of group wants. Nor is it to imply that some form of group representation might not be achieved within other political systems. Nor is it to imply that the role of democratic citizens is or should be only to press their own private wants or interests and the role of democratic governments is or should be only to reconcile those wants. Another strand of democratic theory has insisted on quite the reverse. On this view, the end of democracy is not to secure the systematic representation of interests but to secure the common good. In parallel, the task of citizens and representatives is not to express their self-regarding wants but some conception of the common good.

2. THE COMMON GOOD

Whilst theorists in the utilitarian tradition have pictured the ends of democracy as the satisfaction of private interests or wants, others have seen it as a means of reaching decisions based on conceptions of the common good, not necessarily related to self-regarding wants. Democracy, on this view, is not simply a mechanism through which all citizens can be best assured of their interests being taken into account, but a method of ensuring precisely the opposite, that decisions should be taken by reference to some general social principles. Its aim is not to provide all with opportunities to press partisan claims but to provide all with the opportunity of deliberating and deciding on collective rather than individual goods. Democracy, on this view, is not analogous to a market place in which men meet to strike the best bargain they can with whatever resources they may muster. Rather it is analogous to a forum in which citizens meet to debate and decide what is best for the community as a whole. The task of the political actor (whether he be citizen or representative) is not or not only self-aggrandizement but the reaching of decisions on grounds of general principle. In parallel, the supposed function of a democratic system is to establish the rule of right rather than to achieve the satisfaction of private wants.

This was Rousseau's view. His institutional suggestions were all designed to create an environment in which personal or sectional interests would not be points of reference in the reaching of decisions by the citizen body. He did not see men as essentially or solely altruistic creatures who can be ordinarily relied on to act for others. They will ignore social obligations when self-interest or passion lead them to the breach. Nevertheless, given the proper setting, they can be led to respect communal needs when engaged in law-making. If the community is small, if there are no marked economic or social inequalities, if parties do not confuse the public conscience by introducing partisan feelings into political deliberations, if the decisions on which the citizenry decide are of a general nature and are not applicable only to single persons or particular groups, it can be hoped that men will base their political judgements on some conception of the public good. There are obviously points of contact between this hope and Bentham's expectations of democracy. Like Bentham, Rousseau believed the extension of citizenship would produce decisions based on some general social criteria rather than on the self-regarding wants of rulers; and, like Bentham, he believed a democratic system would achieve this only if citizens were prevented from deciding on public issues on the basis of individual interests or group feelings.[5] That is, both saw democracy as a means of excluding purely individual or sectional wants from the political arena rather than (as many modern theorists suppose) a mechanism for systematically representing them. Nevertheless, there are differences between the two. For Bentham, the exclusion of individual or group interests from the voter's calculations would force him to consider those interests he shared in common with all others. Rousseau insisted too that the citizen should be asked to decide only on laws which could affect him in no way

[5] See W. G. Runciman and A. K. Sen, 'Games, Justice and the General Will' in *Mind* (1965), reprinted in W. G. Runciman, *Sociology in its Place and Other Essays* (Cambridge, 1970), where it is implied that the two positions are identical.

differently than it affected all other citizens; but he implies that
this is a situation in which the citizen can be freed from all
reference to self-interest. It would not be merely that the citizen
could satisfy his own self-interest in no other way than by further-
ing a common interest; it would be that his social judgement
could be released from the bondage of self-interested goals. So the
achievement of democracy is not to utilize efficiently self-interest
in the service of a general interest, but to stimulate civic virtue,
action and judgement based on a concern for the common good.
It would expand the role of public conscience as it whittled away
opportunities for satisfying self-interest. For Benthamites, democracy is the rational political frame for egoists; for Rousseauists,
it is the training ground for altruists.

These expectations were not novel—it had at any rate long
been supposed that a democracy or a republic depended on
the existence of a virtuous citizenry. They might seem now, in
the light of our experience of Western democracies, excessive.
Certainly, Rousseau is treated usually as either the theorist of a
radically different type of system—totalitarian democracy—or a
utopian whose dream of small, homogeneous self-governing communities untainted by the spirit of *parti pris* is quite irrelevant to
present realities or possibilities. Both of these interpretations and
(as they are) criticisms have some foundation. Yet the two different
charges of contributing to the totalitarian tradition and of unreality are consequences of Rousseau's insistence on the possibility
and desirability of complete consensus among the citizenry rather
than of his hope of civic virtue becoming an active principle of
democracy. His emphasis on a common will, connected with his
ideals of freedom and self-government, gives substance to the
accusation that, if his ideas have any present relevance, they
apply to totalitarian systems which do at least claim such unity
rather than to representative democracies in which party and
group competition plays such a major and accepted role. Yet, if
we drop Rousseau's hope that a virtuous citizenry will agree on
the rules that should bind them, if we abandon the implicit assumption that men of good will cannot disagree about general
social principles, we are still left with a model of democracy distant from anything within the utilitarian tradition. For the latter,
a democratic system is the most efficient route to what are taken

to be the general ends of society, the satisfaction of individual interests or wants; for Rousseau and those like him, it is a means of expanding, both in extent and in intensity, civic virtue. For the utilitarian, wants are both egoistic and given, and the problem is how best to satisfy or reconcile them; for Rousseau, human motives are mixed and malleable, and the problem is how to nurture those which develop men as citizens and societies as moral agencies.

Those who see democracy in terms of want-satisfaction can clearly find some comfort in the actual working of Western democracies, which do encourage governmental sensitivity to many if not all wants. The case for Rousseauist hopes might, at first sight, seem to be more flimsy. Yet it is still a question worth asking, how far can a democratic system nurture a concern for the general good? Is there any reason to suppose that the more democratic a political system, the more governments will have to refer in their decisions to some at least claimed general good?

The firmest basis for Rousseauist hopes lies in the fact that a democratic system is likely to publicize political issues. It requires and stimulates debate. It forces on government the necessity of justifying policies, of stating publicly reasons for its actions; and this will almost invariably produce criticisms and counter-proposals. Many now complain about the limitations on debate in Western democracies—the settling of the agenda by the political elites, the secrecy of government, the inaccessibility of the mass media to some brands of opinion. Nevertheless, it would be difficult to deny that public debate is wider, more open and more hotly contested in democratic than in non-democratic systems, or that democratic governments are normally of necessity less secretive and more obliged to speak in self-defence.

Such public debate may have a number of advantages. One is from the viewpoint of want-satisfaction. A situation in which different groups (including government) are obliged to state publicly their positions and to commit themselves openly to future courses of actions might reduce the risks involved in egoistic group action and increase the possibility of mutually satisfactory joint actions. The point can be made clearer by using the familiar Prisoner's Dilemma argument to illustrate the need for trust and communication between rational egoists if they are to achieve advantageous outcomes in situations of conflict. Suppose a two-person situation in which each is faced with two alternatives:

X's alternatives

		a	b
Y's alternatives	c	X wins £5 Y wins £5	X wins £10 Y loses £10
	d	X loses £10 Y wins £10	X loses £5 Y loses £5

If each actor opts for the choice most advantageous to himself (b for X, and d for Y), they will both lose in the outcome (bd). However, if either of the actors choose the other alternative (say Y chooses c), it leaves the way for the other to pick the alternative most favourable to him and least favourable to his opponent (X could choose b, with the outcome bc). Only if the actors trust each other sufficiently to pursue that alternative which might with co-operation produce an outcome favourable to both can an outcome unfavourable to both be avoided. It might be that rational egoists would, in a series of such situations, settle independently on the ac outcome as a matter of enlightened self-interest. But clearly communication between the actors, clarification of the alternatives open to each and of the consequences of their choices, and above all public commitments to future courses of action are likely to ease the development and maintenance of trust and co-operation. Where the options available to political actors are openly discussed, where they may be forced to give public assurances about their future actions—and these situations are likely to be created by open debate—the chances of the non-zero-sum solution being chosen (if such a solution exists) are enhanced.[6]

There may, however, be advantages in public debate other than the better satisfaction of wants. Publicity makes it more likely that governments will have to frame their policies, or at the least defend them, by reference to some general social principles. When discussion and criticism is open, government will of

---

[6] See Anatol Rapaport, *Fights, Games and Debates* (Ann Arbor, 1960), p. 174; Brian Barry, *Political Argument*, pp. 253–5; Robert A. Dahl, *Polyarchy*, pp. 155–6.

necessity have to take into account a number of divergent views and claims. If its policy is especially favourable or unfavourable to particular sections of the community, there will be a pressure on it as the consequence of publicity to justify this discriminatory treatment. One sort of justification will be to refer to the satisfactions which all in the community will receive, in other words will rest on some common interest argument. Or appeal may be made to some greater aggregate of want-satisfaction resulting from the discrimination. Or other social principles, such as justice and equality, may be brought into play. Clearly there can be disagreement on such general principles or on their relevance to the case in point. Nevertheless, it is likely that defence of governmental policy, and also criticism of it, will often be forced to some such level of generality.

These pressures towards general justification may not operate only on government. They may be felt as much by organized groups themselves. At least if their claims are brought into the public arena, interest groups will feel obliged to justify them in some terms other than the wants of their members. If the National Farmers Union presses for higher farm prices or the Association of University Teachers for higher academic salaries, they will seldom give in public justification the bald wish of farmers and academics for more money. The slightest concern for public opinion will quickly spur them into producing more persuasive arguments—the need for a home agriculture in defence terms or to save on the balance of payments, the economic and social benefits flowing from the expansion of higher education, the degree to which farm or academic incomes have slipped in relation to those of comparable groups. The very fact that groups feel the need to present such arguments is some indication that the group model of democracy is insufficient. There is no need to insist on groups' sincerity. Even if they put such cases forward with their tongues in their collective cheeks, they presumably do so in the hope or expectation that it will help their causes, and this implies an appreciation of the importance of a public evaluation of the general merits of their claims. Once such arguments have been stated, moreover, the terms of the problem may change. For it is not then simply a question of government reaching a solution which optimizes the returns to those groups particularly involved, but also of it evaluating the general arguments put and reaching a decision which is itself publicly justifiable.

Although pressure groups may perforce engage in the public debate rather than just expressing wants, they are unlikely to be the main agencies through which a debate on general principles can be sustained. Political parties are the more probable players of this role; and the degree to which a democratic system will stimulate debate rather than aggregate wants will depend heavily on the nature of its parties. Two different views of political parties correspond roughly with the two different analogies of democracy, the forum and the market-place. One view was put most succinctly by Burke: 'Party is a body of men united, for promoting by their joint endeavours the national interest, upon some particular principle in which they are all agreed'. Parallel to this definition of party ran an equally explicit view of the nature of the representative assembly: 'Parliament is not a congress of ambassadors from different and hostile interests . . . but parliament is a *deliberative* assembly of *one* nation, with *one* interest, that of the whole.'[7] Burke's views were never generally accepted even in his own day, and today his definition of party is usually quoted only to be rejected. A more accepted view of party now would be a body of men aiming at public office whose *modus operandi* will be the aggregation of the votes of sectional groups and whose function will in consequence be, at least in the more developed democratic systems, the aggregation of interests. In this sense, parties perform at a pre-governmental level what is regarded as a function parallel to that of government itself, the integration and reconciliation of group demands into a limited range of policy alternatives. In the democratic division of labour, organized groups articulate interests and claims, whilst parties aggregate those interests and claims. The pragmatic, bargaining party rather than the value-oriented, ideological party is thus typical of and necessary to the stable democracies.[8]

Of course those who define parties in terms of interest aggre-

[7] 'Thoughts on the Causes of the Present Discontents' in *The Works of the Right Hon. Edmund Burke* (2 vols., London, 1854), vol. I, p. 151. 'Speech to the Electors of Bristol, November 1774' in ibid., p. 180.

[8] See, for example, the discussion in G. A. Almond and J. S. Coleman, *The Politics of Developing Areas* (Princeton, 1960), pp. 33–45.

gation would not want necessarily to represent this as the only function of parties in a liberal democracy nor to commit themselves openly to a preference for this type of party rather than those more ideologically based. Nevertheless, there has been a certain measure of accord in seeing the 'pragmatic' party as peculiarly appropriate to a pluralistic society, since it alone can achieve what is taken to be the democratic objective, the satisfaction of group wants.

Despite this accord, the Burkean view of party is not necessarily without contemporary relevance in either normative or descriptive terms. Normatively, the pragmatic party is only appropriate to a democracy if democracy is seen in want-satisfaction terms; if it is seen rather as promoting debate on the public good, the value-oriented ideological party would be the more suitable agent of democracy. Empirically, it is by no means clear that the bargaining model is entirely appropriate, at any rate in party systems other than the American. There does seem to be a consistent under-valuation of the role of ideology in determining party behaviour by acting as either a constraint on or an incentive towards particular actions. What needs to be noticed is that, however accurate the depiction of parties in existing democracies as pragmatic and bargaining, the acceptance of this type of party as somehow appropriate involves a particular and contestable view of the ends of a democratic system. On another view, ideologically divided parties, capable of sustaining a debate on political principles, might be necessary if democracy is to fulfil its promise.

3. LIBERTY

One defence of democracy, indeed of any form of representative government, has been that it is a means of safeguarding the liberty of subjects, of protecting them against unnecessary or arbitrary constraints on their actions. A system of popular elections and representative bodies will effectively secure against governmental tyranny and oppression. This Whig (or in American terms Jeffersonian) view is essentially negative; the counter to oppressive government is to make the process of governing difficult and the task of the 'popular' elements of a constitution is to act as a restraint on government. In this scenario, the part of the people is to set the limits of government action rather than to determine its content. Accountability is valuable because it is a powerful antidote to the corrupting effect of power.

There are two implications of this Whig view. Firstly, a government subject to popular control will be less extensive in its field of operation than any kind of authoritarian government. Secondly, whatever the scope of government regulation, responsible government will be less arbitrary in its actions than other systems.

These assumptions might be questioned. The first runs up against the fact that the development of democracy in Europe and America has historically coincided with a very general increase in the regulatory powers of government. This might of course be purely fortuitous. Even so, it could be argued that there are pressures within a democracy leading to increased government intervention and that the people is not often content with its Lockean role of resisting abuses and the over-extension of power. Clearly the growth of democracy might bring into a position of political influence groups whose priorities are different from men in the Lockean mould. The poor are likely to be interested in equality or at least in greater measures of social welfare, both more capable of being provided through public than private action. Many, apart from the poor, in a complex modern economy might demand of government that it should provide at least economic stability and job security and at most continuous economic growth. The ends that men may wish government to satisfy are neither uniform nor static, and certainly they cannot be comprehended under the Whig rubric of order and freedom. There is no reason to suppose, perhaps good reason to doubt, that a responsible government will be necessarily less liable to sacrifice liberty to other ends than other forms of government.

It may be too that a democratic government can more easily increase the range of its operations since it can claim a greater degree of legitimacy than most, or at any rate its decisions will be accepted as legitimate by its citizens. Tocqueville long ago pointed out the fallacy in the Whig view of representative bodies as insti-

tutionalized expressions of the popular right of resistance, the
liberal organ of permanent revolution. The view ignores the
psychological effects of popular control, the general acceptance
of democratic government as acting on the wishes of the people
or at least of the majority. In this context, resistance to extensions
of government power is difficult since it seems to amount to resistance to popular decision, or at the most the rightness of such
extensions is likely to be contested only on the grounds that they
are not really desired by the majority. Psychologically, resentment of government performance, or at any rate the transforma-
tion of that resentment into sustained opposition to the regime, is
always likely to be weakened by the argument that government
stands for the whole people whilst dissidents stand only for themselves.

Another ground for doubting the Whig identification of democracy and limited government, as we have seen central to much
recent discussion of democracy, is the decline of faith in the
liberal propensities of the masses. At the root of Whig doctrine is
the assumption that the mass of men want freedom. If this
assumption is mistaken, if many are afraid of freedom and attracted by the comforting certainties authoritarian government
can provide, a democratic means may not be the way to a liberal
end.

The Whig and Jeffersonian expectation that democracy would
erect barriers to the extension of governmental power may then
be ill-founded. Is the assumption that democratic representative
institutions will provide against arbitrary actions in any better
case? Do representative bodies provide effective protection for
individual citizens against arbitrary actions by government or
bureaucracy? Again the case could be put that less and less can
such bodies effectively perform this historic role. Of course, even
in Whig theory, the expression and remedy of individual grievances by representatives was not seen as the only source of protection for the citizen—the rule of law, the subjection of officials
to the ordinary law and courts of the land even while performing
their official functions, was another. Nevertheless, the present
concern with finding other or additional means of protecting the
citizen against administrative abuses and arbitrariness—means
such as the Ombudsman or bills of rights—does suggest that

democratic representation is at least not now generally regarded as a sufficient constraint upon large and complex governmental bureaucracies.

There may then be good reasons for questioning the identification of democracy and 'limited' or 'liberal' government. Nevertheless, even though we should guard against the over-easy supposition that democracies will necessarily assure a wide area of individual liberty and necessarily eradicate the insolence of office, there may be equally good reasons for accepting the Whig argument at least in a muted form. Although responsible government and widespread political participation may not guarantee liberal measures, a democratic regime is likely to prove more hospitable than other regimes to a liberal stance.

To some extent, the connection is a necessary one. Certain freedoms are essential to the maintenance of any kind of responsible government. Most obviously, no accountability could be maintained if freedom of speech and freedom of association were not protected. In this respect, the institutional and legal conditions necessary to democracy do coincide with classical liberal requirements.

A causal connection is more doubtful. Here the criticisms of the Whig view seem justified. Where governmental intervention is favoured by a majority or influential sections of the people (and this is not improbable), a democratic system may well encourage increased intervention. This obvious possibility is somewhat obscured by our tendency to compare Western democracies with totalitarian systems, in which the extent of control over the individual is by definition wide. However, if we compare Britain and America, not with Russia or China, but with say Portugal or Brazil, we might be less persuaded that the area of governmental control is necessarily commensurate with the degree of democracy. This comparison points to the root of the difficulty in establishing the relationship between democracy and government intervention. Plausibly the most significant factor in determining levels of government intervention is the level of economic development. The more complex the economy, the more pressing will be the need for political regulation. But, as we have already seen, there is also a significant association between level of economic development or level of modernization and the ability to maintain a stable democracy. It becomes in consequence difficult to disentangle the effects on levels of intervention of the type of regime and of levels of economic development.[9]

To this extent, the Whig identification of responsible and limited government is doubtful or at least unproven. However, if we turn from the extent of government intervention to the oppressiveness of government policies, there may be a good deal more substance in the Whig case. At any rate, it seems plausible that, where there is some approximate political equality, severe oppression of minority groups is less likely. The point must be made again that even minorities possessing the vote may be excluded from influence, if they are in a permanent minority or if the distribution of political resources is highly unequal. But, given a situation of rough equality, minorities will generally have sufficient political leverage to afford some self-protection. It seems likely that democratic regimes will be debarred from an extensive use of extreme coercion at least against its own population. It is difficult to imagine such a regime being able to utilize massive physical power to force through policies as did Stalin in his forced collectivization programme and his purges of the 'thirties, or as did Hitler in his extermination of the Jews. In this sense, democratic governments might be more sensitive than other regimes to violent challenge because of the constraints placed on them in resorting to counter-violence.

Representative organs may be proving an insufficient defence against administrative abuses or arbitrariness, but it is nevertheless probable that a democratic regime will be more likely than other systems to sustain a concern over such abuses and to create institutions to curtail them. Again publicity is all-important. Muck-raking may be sporadic in its incidence and sensational in its intent, but it does provide some safeguard against bureaucratic abuse. And representative bodies as well as the press can give publicity to individual grievances.

The Whig defence of responsible government has then a residual truth. One major assumption made in that defence is unsound. It is not the case that democratic governments necessarily preside over the night-watchman state, securing the mini-

[9] It is not of course impossible provided that some operationally effective indices of levels of intervention could be constructed.

mal possible functions at the lowest cost in monetary terms and in terms of restrictions on individual action. Nevertheless, the popular control over government implicit in a democratic structure is possibly one of the securest safeguards against the grossest forms of oppression to which governments are prone.

4. PARTICIPATION

Criticisms of revisionist or empirical theorists of democracy have on the whole started from a charge of moral obtuseness. The revisionists have, in producing a theory purporting to fit the practice of Western democracies, lost sight of the fundamental values towards which democratic theory has traditionally strained. Covertly they have produced a justification for those systems from which the democratic content has been drained.

Such criticism has often incorporated an attack on the now notorious dictum of Schumpeter that democracy is merely 'a political *method*, that is to say, a certain type of institutional arrangement for arriving at political—legislative and administrative—decisions and hence incapable of being an end in itself, irrespective of what decisions it will produce under given historical conditions'.[10] As against this, radical theorists assert that democracy is not just a method, not just a means of assuring or at least maximizing desirable governmental outputs, and thus dependent on providing that service to other ideals for its justification. The democratic process is an end-in-itself in that it requires or rather means the maximum possible participation of all citizens in the activity of public decision-making.

Posing the disagreement in these means/ends terms has probably served only to confuse it. With qualifications, Schumpeter accepts that the democratic method is justifiable because it is likely to achieve governmental results desirable on some ideal grounds. Although he himself does not attempt the task, it would be reasonable therefore to expect a democratic theory to specify the ends to be achieved and to give some reasons (empirical or logical or both) for supposing these ends will be served by democracy at least more effectively than by alternative systems. On the

10 Joseph A. Schumpeter, op. cit., p. 242.

other hand, in assessing the radical claims, it is not clear that participation can stand as an end-in-itself. It is possible of course for a theorist to take his stand on political equality as an ultimate good, but traditionally and contemporaneously participatory theorists have seen it as a way in which other ends, say the development of the individual, can be furthered. In which case, democracy is a means to them as much as to Schumpeter.

We are not then concerned with dividing those who regard democracy as a means from those who see it as an end. Nor are we concerned with distinguishing between those with some special claim to scientific modernity from those clinging to the old, traditional, radical truths. The differences derive from different emphases about the goods to be achieved by a democracy. On the one side, democracy is justifiable in terms of the quality and nature of the governmental decisions that emerge from it. The standards against which those decisions are measured—social utility, the common good, the satisfaction of actual wants, the assurance of a broad area of liberty—have varied from one theorist to another; what has been accepted in common is that the virtues of a political system are measurable in terms of governmental performance. On the other side is the view that the virtues of a polity are bound up with its effects on the characters of its citizens. The concern was expressed most clearly by Mill: 'the most important point of excellence which any form of government can possess is, to promote the virtue and intelligence of the people themselves'.[11]

From this standpoint, the educative function of a political system is at least as important as its decision-making function; and the attractions of democracy are not, or not only, that it is a mechanism making for better government but that it creates an environment making for better men. Clearly, neither of these views has an exclusive claim to a long intellectual lineage. 'Traditional' theorists have seen democracy in good government terms as well as in educative terms. Indeed some have embraced both modes of justification; Rousseau saw it as a way of assuring government in accordance with the general good as well as a means of moralizing men, whilst John Stuart Mill hoped that it

[11] 'Representative Government' in *Utilitarianism, Liberty and Representative Government* (Everyman ed., 1944), p. 193.

would both guarantee negative liberty and provide expanded opportunities for active citizenship. Equally clearly, neither of these justificatory positions has any exclusive claim to scientific respectability, although of course it could well be the case that one might empirically be demonstrated to provide a more appropriate justification of existing democracies than the other.

The two modes of justification reflect two even more basic judgements of the worth and purpose of political life. For the first, political activity is instrumental in the sense that it is undertaken only to secure the satisfaction of other individual needs. It is to be counted as a cost, a burden, which can be offset only by the benefits the individual might derive from government action. Engagement in such activity finds its return in the shaping of government policies to the wishes or interests of the citizen-actors. This attitude towards participation is an outgrowth of earlier contractual views of the state and political obligation. In their different ways, both Hobbes and Locke saw civil society as an artifact, a creation of individual wills, agreed in the construction of a social order allowing each one of them to achieve purposes anterior and morally prior to the society itself. Social obligations are thus the price rational men are willing to pay to secure ends, such as security of person or property, of which they can conceive as isolated, asocial individuals. Translated into democratic terminology, citizenship is seen as a means of satisfying private wants and exclusion from citizenship carries with it solely the danger that the wants of the excluded may be ignored. If those wants are satisfied without engagement in public activity, so much the better, for then satisfactions carry no costs at all. This is the basis for contemporary defences of apathy. If men are apathetic, if voting is low and political involvement is both esoteric and lukewarm, all is well, for such apathy demonstrates contentment with governmental outcomes and a suitable concentration on a private sphere, the enrichment of which is the prime purpose of the political system in general and democracy in particular. At its worst, this attitude combines an exaggerated cynicism towards the public world with an equally gross sentimentality towards private life. Politics is, to quote a well-known title, 'who gets what, when, how'. The private life—the insulated life of family, lovers and friends—is in contrast where men can find their real selves, where they are or can become whatever they are actually or potentially at their fullest.

The alternative is that political engagement is not simply a sacrifice made to satisfy wants, safeguard interests or protect liberty, but is itself enriching. It is valuable because to be a citizen, to be a man acting upon a public stage, is to be a better man, to extend capacities and achievements by moving in a public dimension inaccessible to the purely private person. Withdrawal from public endeavour and activity could, on this view, never be justified on the grounds that the right to participate is derivable from the right to have actual wants taken into account or that the obligation to participate is contingent merely upon wants not being satisfied. Both the right and the obligation rest on the supposition that citizenship enlarges and improves the lives of individuals, not by enabling them to shackle collective power to their individual ends but by engaging them as communal persons in the life of the community.

This is to put the independent value of participation in its largest terms. When looked at in more detail, this simplicity dissolves and the justificatory arguments for participation take on a number of different shapes. Extensive popular participation in politics might be demanded as a means towards a number of different ends, even if these ends are to do with the individual citizen rather than with governmental outputs. It is important to distinguish these alternative arguments, if only because they can lead to different demands in terms of institutional arrangements.

One ground for the extension of citizenship in these terms is that it constitutes the social recognition of the moral and intellectual worth and dignity of the individual. To allow or encourage universal entry into the political community is to recognize all men as sources of values and to accept in consequence that each has a right to be consulted and play a part in the social allocation of values. The point here is not that every person or group has interests to be defended or wants to be satisfied but that all (with very limited exceptions) are capable of making judgements worthy of being taken into account in public deliberations. Incorporation into the political community is both justified by this assertion and is a recognition of its truth.

This idea of citizenship as a stamp denoting communal ack-

nowledgement of individual worth has historically provided probably the strongest emotional thrust towards democracy. The force
of its appeal found expression in the Putney Debates with Colonel
Rainboro's plea, 'The poorest he that is in England hath a life
to live as the richest he.' British working class radical demands in
the nineteenth century were powered by the same insistence that
individual worth was not to be measured by social position and
that the right to vote was an affirmation of worth. Of course,
much of this argument was put in representation of interests
terms. Working-class interests could never be properly attended
to unless working men had the vote and working men appeared
in Parliament. But another, no less deeply felt, plea ran parallel
—we are men as other men and deserve no less a place or opportunity in public life. If these moral deserts were not obvious, it
was up to working men to demonstrate them; which is at least a
part explanation of the close association, particularly amongst
the working class leadership, of the temperance movement and
nonconformity with radical politics. In the same way, the demand
for working-class M.P.s, labour representation, which started in
the 1820s and culminated in the formation of the Labour Representation Committee, was not urged simply as a defence of class
interests but was as much an assertion of class dignity.

A less dramatic but perhaps more apposite example of the force
of the idea of the vote as an acknowledgement of social existence
is presented by recent reductions of the age of voting. The common and very often successful pressure to bring down the age
below twenty-one has relied almost wholly on arguments cast in
this mould. Clearly, it is difficult to present any firm case that 18
to 21 year olds have peculiar wants or interests, distinguishable
for instance from those of 21 to 24 year olds, which need assert-
ing and protecting through the electoral process. In consequence,
the justificatory argument has been presented almost wholly in
terms of deserts. Eighteen-year olds are mature enough, or have
extensive enough social obligations, to merit incorporation as
actors in the political community. In other words, the arguments
have largely revolved around the age of initiation into adulthood.
In societies which have few other initiation ceremonies with a
generally accepted symbolic meaning, the argument is invested
with even greater emotional weight.

To participate is then to have one's individual worth recognized. To be an actor and not merely acted upon is in itself a sustaining acknowledgement of moral stature. However, this is only one of the available justifications of popular participation as a route to the improvement of mankind. Another has been expressed in the persistent association of democracy with 'self-government'. The value of participation to the individual from this standpoint lies in the possibility it opens of his determining the social rules that are to bind him; and the most consistent advocate of the view has been Rousseau.

Rousseau, it has been claimed, sought a political system which would direct men away from individual aims and towards collective aims. He sought also for a system which would encourage the emergence and expression of a moral consensus and enthrone this as the determinant of social rules. The connecting link between these ideas and between both and the notion of self-government was his concept of freedom. This, to repeat, consisted in 'obedience to a law which we prescribe to ourselves'. The definition had two separate implications. One, foreshadowing the Kantian ethic, was that men are unfree when they are not following a rule of behaviour, when their actions are unconsidered and unrelated to any universalizable principle. The other, more relevant to his political theory, was that they are unfree if the rules they follow are prescribed to them by others. The second implication does not divide Rousseau sharply from a liberal such as John Stuart Mill; he too would have accepted that men are unfree to the degree they are restricted by politically or socially imposed rules. The difference lies in Mill's consequent acceptance of some such restriction as an entailment of an ordered social life and Rousseau's absolute rejection of any such limitation. Rousseau's object was, he said, in a phrase which is something more than off-hand hyperbole, to find 'a form of association . . . in which each, while uniting himself with all, may still obey himself alone, and remain as free as before'.[12] Full freedom was attainable even in a regulated society, and it would be attained when all the social rules governing individuals were accepted by each one of them. Full freedom was then identical with complete self-

[12] *The Social Contract and Discourses* (Everyman ed., 1947), p. 12.

government and this, Rousseau believed, would emerge within his face-to-face democracy. As we have seen, this ambition involves him in the problem of unanimity, a problem he attempts to solve by presupposing a potential moral consensus within the community which, given the right institutional environment, can manifest itself in the general will.

The unreality of this presupposition flaws Rousseau's democratic theory and undermines the ideal of participation as a route to self-government. Let us say all that can be said in his support. We might admit that rough equality of possessions and similarity of life-styles, which he saw as social conditions necessary to self-government, would tend to encourage moral agreement. Homogeneity of attitudes and moral conformity might be more likely in small than in large communities. Disagreement might be lessened if men could be encouraged or even forced to judge issues from a collective standpoint rather than through a consideration of their own interests. It seems highly likely that a 'civil religion' imposed by the state would, as Rousseau thought, be a powerful support of social unity. In a word, Rousseau did suggest some social and institutional conditions conducive to the consensus his self-government ideal requires. In view of the many attacks upon him as the progenitor of modern dictatorships, it should also be remembered that the faith in a moral order perceptible to all rational men, or men consulting their consciences or their common sense aright, was a commonplace of his age, indeed of most ages except our own. Having said all this in defence, it must still be admitted that Rousseau's hopes for a consensus are exaggerated, even if the conditions he saw as necessary were established. With Marx, he believed moral and political discord to be a consequence of faulty, and thus remediable or at least transitory, social arrangements. Once the conflicts of interest encouraged by faulty arrangements were diminished or abolished, a modulation into moral harmony would at last be possible. More sceptically than Marx, Rousseau continued in the belief that, although men could in common appreciate the right course and could therefore agree on social rules, they might subsequently be tempted by interest or passion to break them; and in consequence government, forcing men to be free, would still be necessary. Nevertheless he shared the root anarchist belief that men can achieve self-government through moral conformity.

Even if such a consensus were possible (and we might unfortunately be in a better position than Rousseau to imagine techniques for reaching it), it would still be a matter of debate whether or not it is desirable. If 'self-government' requires the claustrophobic intellectual stability and moral conformity apparently necessary to it, is it a political end highly to be desired? Would some restriction of our freedom in Rousseau's sense, some governance by rules to which we have not agreed, be too great a sacrifice for the maintenance of some intellectual and moral independence or even eccentricity?

Some democratic theorists, no less concerned than Rousseau with the extension of political participation, would have replied with an emphatic negative. Indeed, for Tocqueville and John Stuart Mill, the very point of a broadening of participation was to avoid what they saw as an imminent danger of social conformity. Far from welcoming democracy as a means of inaugurating an age of perfect concord, they saw it primarily as a possible context in which men could retain their self-identity and individuality, their self-respect and self-assertiveness, seriously threatened by the trends of the time towards moral and intellectual consensus. Both these thinkers saw democracy as a means towards a social pluralism that would complement if not supersede the constitutional pluralism central to older limited government theories. For both too democracy serves another and perhaps wider purpose. It allows men to develop themselves as social men, to maintain and extend a commitment to public activity, activity aimed at affecting public policies and through them the shape and nature of communal life. Both saw politics in a heroic, classical mode. The point of the political life is not solely to defend congeries of interests, nor to ensure self-government, nor even to preserve a wide area of personal liberty. It is to provide a stage on which men can enact a public role. In a sense, the public performance is self-sufficient, with no need of justification in terms of government outputs. Or, at any rate, if it requires further vindication, this can be found in the beneficial effects the performance has on the characters of the actors.

What are these benefits? Firstly and most importantly, it seems, participation in political life stimulates the active rather than the passive character. Non-democratic and democratic systems, said Mill, encourage and require two different types of character and our decisions on political forms must take into account which is the more desirable, 'that which struggles against evils, or that which endures them; that which bends to circumstances, or that which endeavours to make circumstances bend to itself'. On intellectual, practical and moral grounds equally, the choice was clear to Mill. All intellectual progress, whether individual or collective, is linked to some serious attempt to explain and affect the real world; practical achievement is never the fruit of passivity; and, above all, apathy and the withdrawal from active effort is rarely a moral virtue, more often hiding sullen discontent and envy than revealing a humble disavowal of aggression or self-interest.[18] Tocqueville committed himself to much the same ideals of character. His most pressing fear for the future was that men would be reduced to the status of social 'colonists', accepting whatever services society might provide for them but unable or unwilling to intervene actively in its running. Like Mill too he saw the moral advantage to lie with the proud and active rather than the humble and passive. 'Moralists are constantly complaining that the dominant vice of our age is pride ... Far from thinking that humility should be preached to our contemporaries, I wish some attempt might be made to give them a more exalted view of themselves and their species; to my mind what they need to keep them healthy is not humility but pride.'[14]

Both believed democratic participation would stimulate not only the active character but also a particular and desirable mode of action. In a dictatorial or hierarchical society, co-ordination can be achieved partly through the apathy and powerlessness of the masses, partly through the physical power or social influence available to leadership. In a democracy, much effective action must necessarily be based on voluntary co-operation. Put another way, this means that leadership will rest essentially on the arts of persuasion, and those who wish for influence must learn those arts. To the degree that political

13 J. S. Mill, op. cit., pp. 211–14.
14 Alexis de Tocqueville, *Oeuvres complètes* (ed. J. P. Mayer, Paris, 1951–), vol. i (ii), p. 255.

K

equality is established, older disciplines and weapons of influence —physical strength, wealth, status—will decline relatively as instruments of leadership. What will be left are essentially the skills of the orator. The replacement of coercion by persuasion is again, from this viewpoint, to be welcomed not only because it creates more responsive government, but because it adds to the stature and capacities both of those who follow and those who would wield influence. To those who are to follow it acknowledges and calls upon their powers of judgement; from those who seek to lead, it demands force of argument and example rather than the force of arms or wealth. The more active and the more general is the engagement in public affairs, the less likely is mere demagogy to be the route to political success.

The last beneficial effect of participatory democracy on character is its nurturing and diffusing of a largeness of view and a breadth of vision inaccessible to the many under other forms of government. When the private citizen is engaged in public functions, argued Mill, 'he is called . . . to weigh interests not his own; to be guided, in case of conflicting claims, by another rule than his private partialities; to apply, at every turn, principles and maxims which have for their reason of existence the common good . . . Where this school of public spirit does not exist, scarcely any sense is entertained that private persons, in no eminent social situation, owe any duties to society, except to obey the laws and submit to the government.'[15] Tocqueville too spoke the same language of civic education. Constantly he referred to democratic institutions as schools in which men could learn to rise above narrow, self-interested aims and to place the good of society as well as the interests of others into the account when balancing public policies. A devotion to public good could not be expected from the purely private person.

Clearly, it would be sanguine to expect an active, co-operative and public-spirited civic character to result merely from voting in elections at infrequent intervals. Tocqueville and Mill did not expect it—which is why they placed so much emphasis on institutions other than those of central government. For democracy to exert its beneficial effects on character, it was necessary for men to be involved personally in social issues and organiza-

[15] J. S. Mill, op. cit., p. 217.

tions, to assume directly and not just vicariously public functions. Obviously, the degree to which this is possible is related to the size of the association. This is why participatory theorists have always been concerned with the problem of scale, for the bigger the organization or political unit the less possible it is for it to permit those forms of participation essential to the character-building purposes, the educative purposes, of democracy. Rousseau's perhaps illusory answer was to limit the size of the state. Tocqueville and Mill looked to the democratization and politicization of those small-scale associations in which individuals could play a significant role. This led them to place great weight on, for instance, local self-government and the jury system as ways in which citizens could be directly integrated in the work of the public administration. It explains too why they were, and especially Tocqueville, extremely concerned with the development of voluntary associations mediating between the citizenry and the political leadership.

The relationship between social pluralism and democracy has become at the present time one of the most persistently discussed aspects of democratic theory, and this makes it the more necessary to disentangle the various different forms this relationship might take. In particular, the relation between pluralism and participation is not straightforward. On the one side not all participatory theorists have welcomed social pluralism, whilst on the other democratic theorists who welcome social pluralism have not always done so on participatory grounds. Since we have looked at Rousseau's view of participation, the first point needs no extensive elaboration. Rousseau certainly did not see a plurality of associations as a desirable feature of his participatory democracy. They could only prove divisive and hinder the emergence of that consensual agreement necessary to self-government. If such associations had to exist, it would be better for them to be as numerous as possible since this would weaken their influence and lessen their encouragement of organized dissidence.

The second point, that social pluralism can be defended on both participatory and non-participatory grounds, needs perhaps more emphasis. In one of the most sustained recent attacks on 'democratic elitists', Peter Bachrach places Tocqueville as the founding father of this tendentious redefinition of democracy and attacks the current identification of democracy and social pluralism.[16] The danger with this kind of undifferentiated attack is that it can obscure possible connections between social pluralism and participatory ambitions. Group formations and group politics can be defended on grounds of want-satisfaction; these are the means by which all wants or all strong wants can be forced into the political reckoning. However, they can be defended also as a means by which large numbers can be involved actively in the determination of public policies and in a concern for public issues. It was largely on these grounds that Tocqueville welcomed voluntary associations.

The argument has some obvious defects if offered as a justification of group activity in Western democracies. In the first place, it shares a difficulty with the justification of group activity in want-satisfaction terms. This is the inadequate coverage which group membership actually achieves. Generally, the higher the social class, the higher is the incidence of group membership. Tocqueville's schools of civic education are not then by any means comprehensive.

Secondly, membership of organized groups does not always imply active involvement in their running. There may be a tendency in such groups for the leadership or the bureaucracy effectively to monopolize the administration and the policy-determination of the group. The activism of group members may also be related to social class. These possibilities present no insuperable difficulties to defenders of pluralism in want-satisfaction terms. For elite domination of groups can be justified in the same way as elite domination of a democratic system. Membership apathy is a demonstration of the satisfactory performance by the leadership of their function, the representation of group wants. No such escape, of course, is available to those who justify pluralism on participatory grounds.

It may, thirdly, be doubtful if the type of groups which dominate group activity in Western democracies are likely to encourage the characteristics seen by Mill and Tocqueville as the benefits of participation. If we distinguish interest groups from cause groups, that is those pressing the interests of their members from those pressing for particular public policies on grounds of

[16] Peter Bachrach, op. cit., pp. 26, 36–7, 42–5.

some general social principle or altruistic purpose, the importance of interest groups and the comparative unimportance of cause groups in the political process is very apparent. And it may be doubted if interest groups are adequate training grounds for the broadness of vision desired by Tocqueville and Mill.

For these several reasons, the educative effects of participation can only with difficulty count as a strong justification of present group activities. Or, at any rate, it would have to be conceded that such a justification can only be brought into play to the degree that voluntary associations do in fact involve their members in administrative and decision-making functions. From this point of view, the success of social pluralism in contributing to democratic ends is not measurable by the efficacy of its representation and protection of interests, but by the extent to which it offers a real experience of ruling and being ruled. It is not perhaps a simple coincidence that, despite the growth of group studies into a minor industry, comparatively little empirical research has been undertaken into the authority structures of pressure groups and voluntary associations. Yet it is just such research that would be relevant to any full account of the democratic functions of such groups.

The participatory defence of social pluralism may not then fit easily on to present democratic practice. It may be too that the emphasis on the central importance of voluntary associations has led some pluralists to neglect those associations in which men are enrolled involuntarily, work associations, but which may nevertheless be a much more vital and formative experience to them as individuals. Whatever the educative work of tennis clubs and trade unions, societies for the protection of this or the abolition of that, whatever the character-building effects of local self-government and jury service, these influences are likely to affect the individual less than the workplace. If participation in decision-making is a crucial element in civic education, participation in the decisions most intimately and consistently governing everyday life are likely to be the most crucial. And still, in present society, the work experience is one of the most decisive formative factors in the development of most individuals. Late in life John Stuart Mill did in fact touch on these consequences of his participatory ideal, but their exploration has largely been the work of socialists such as G. D. H. Cole whose socialism (at least in his early writings) consisted not in advocacy of state ownership and management of industry but in the idea of worker ownership and control. With the recent revival of interest in participation as a democratic ideal, democratic theorists have again turned to the question of democracy in industry.[17] The same ideological gloss can be put on other recent demands for student participation in university government and for the extension of community power.

Whatever the different institutional recommendations and lines of empirical research which may be prompted by the present concern with the ideal of participation, we can trace its major constituents in the mainstream of democratic theory. Attachment to this ideal leads to a concern not with the performance of democratic governments but with the civic experience a democratic polity offers. If the experience is to be meaningful, individual citizens must be personally involved in some demanding and rewarding social functions and, since only a few can be more than marginally involved in the management of a large modern state, the problem of size has been the most difficult participatory theorists have had to face. One response, that of Rousseau, has been to seek the diminution of the state. A probably more fruitful response has been to seek for participation in areas of decision-making other than and more accessible to citizens than that of national government. The one response has led to the rejection of social pluralism, the other to its ardent acceptance as the means to a more extended participation. This divergence amongst participatory theorists has been strengthened by different conceptions of the experience that participation can provide. For Rousseau it was experience in self-government, not just in the sense of playing an active role in public life but in the stricter sense of determining the social rules binding one. In consequence, the object of political education was the quiescence of complete co-operation and agreement. Democracy at its most valuable would express and allow for harmony not discord, silence not debate. To Tocqueville and Mill, on the contrary, the value of the

[17] G. D. H. Cole, *Self-Government in Industry* (1919); Peter Bachrach, op. cit., Chapter 7; Carole Pateman, op. cit., Chapter IV; Robert A. Dahl, *After the Revolution?*, pp. 115-40.

participatory experience lies in its encouraging men to exercise an independent judgement, enabling and even forcing them to take public stands on public issues, stimulating a political dialectic which, even if it does not result in improved policies, at least results in improved persons. A participatory society would foster disagreement and, given all the dangers of social conformity, this was its most attractive promise.

There are then differences between participatory theories of democracy, differences that focus on reactions to social pluralism and to the relation between the state and other forms of association. At the same time, social pluralism is defensible, or is at any rate defended, on want-satisfaction as well as on participatory grounds. Here the divergence lies in the features of associations regarded as most vital to a democratic system, in the one case the expression of members' wants, in the other the involvement of members in the organizational life of the association.

Five

CONCLUSION

Two alternative strategies towards inquiry into democracy were posed in the Introduction, the analytic and the empirical. The first, it has been argued, must have a prior claim over the second. No definition of democracy can be found by gazing at the real world, no matter how meticulous the inspection. And theories of democracy, although they can be tested by empirical investigation, cannot in the last resort be derived from it. Even to identify what are to be the objects of empirical research, we must have in mind some notion of what the operative principle of democracy is. That principle, it has been held here, is political equality.

Given this starting-point, we have a lever with which we can begin to move the real world. Democracies are those systems which at least comparatively approach a situation of equality. Inevitably, the real world will offer only approximations to the ideal or the ideal type. There may be all sorts of unavoidable barriers to political equality. Human nature may be one. If differences in political aptitudes are endemic amongst men, inequalities of influence could survive any institutional rearrangement. Inequalities may be inevitable in any form of political association, for some specialization of function and some ordination may be necessary in any organization, no matter how small. It may be too that some features of modern industrial society present peculiar obstacles to equality of influence. Nevertheless, systems can vary in the degree to which they approach equality. The degree is measurable by the extent to which all groups can play a role in communal decision-making, the extent to which governmental decisions are subject to popular control and the extent to which ordinary men and women are involved in the running of the community, in public administration in the widest sense.

In this light, the term democracy can be used as a neutral term of classification. But it serves as a beacon as well as a torch. The continuum of monopoly, oligopoly and equality can be used to typify political systems. It can be used also, and no less legitimately, to distinguish the desirable from the undesirable. The dual role is unavoidable. If systems are to be defined in terms of operative principles, those principles can be taken as objectives as well as classificatory concepts. It would be futile to suppose that perfect detachment can be achieved when we talk of a subject so charged as democracy. Further still, normative neutrality is an overinflated virtue if all that is meant by it is that the academic should not let his feelings show or should not hold to any too obviously practical a purpose or should be willing as a matter of academic duty to serve any political ends. The danger is that the claim to scientific neutrality can cover an uncritical disregard for actual normative assumptions, particularly those involved in the choice of problems for empirical investigation. The concern of much recent research with the stability of democracies is an example of such unconscious assertion of normative positions. Only the accompanying assumption that systems move automatically back to some equilibrium point has allowed this concern to be dressed in the guise of scientific objectivity.

The move from a statement of operative principles to the discovery of the institutions embodying them is a difficult one. It cannot be made without consideration of the concrete circumstances of particular cases. The ways in which all groups can achieve a political influence, popular control over government can be established and wide participation in public administration can be encouraged are various and will differ with the social structure and political traditions of different communities. It is then hard to state with any precision what institutions or practices are necessary to democracy. Some conditions of responsible government can be asserted with fair assurance—wide freedom of association, freedom of speech and free elections. Other conditions will usually be necessary—a majority decision procedure and a responsible party system in the sense that responsibility for governmental performance can be pinned on to particular political groups and the electorate can choose between real policy alternatives. Beyond this, the degree to which political equality is present (or, from a normative standpoint, the ways in which it can be enhanced) is a matter of weighing the specific effects of the institutions and practices of particular communities.

Of course, the normative problem of defining appropriate institutions does not stop there. Most obviously the claims of democracy have to be balanced against other ends. If more democracy would diminish the decisiveness of government action or result in less informed or more volatile decisions, if more democracy would provoke political instability, if more democracy would weaken the industrial base of modern society, more democracy might be undesirable. The awkward choice between equally laudable but mutually incompatible political ends cannot always be avoided.

The choice of appropriate institutions will depend also on what we want from democracy. This is the best defence of a closer examination of 'normative' theories of democracy than is presently fashionable in political studies. To take only one possible alternative, the greatest satisfaction of wants will suggest a different set of arrangements than the encouragement of active citizenship. Of course, so long as these ends are both supposed to result from democracy, they will suggest some institutions in common. The point is that the choice of one end rather than the other will result in different emphasis when we look at, for instance, questions of local government organizations or the proper role and structure of pressure groups.

Even if it is concerned with some perennial problems of human organization, political theory is moved by changing historical currents. The debate on democracy has been affected, many would say resuscitated, by the often violent dislocation of apparently stable democracies over the last decade. Political scientists have been belaboured because they did not foresee this disruption before the event, perhaps unfairly since few of them would claim the gift of specific prophecy. But, if they cannot foretell the future, they should respond to a changing present. To some degree they have done so, for recent criticism of revisionist theories is just such a response. Some parts of the revisionist structure have become too shaky to bear much weight. Plainly, stability is not achieved through some self-adjusting capacity of existing systems; and, if we cannot rely on some *deus ex machina*, we must perforce rely on ourselves. In other words, the stability of democracies must be worked for; it is a political end like other political ends to be realized through conscious action. Equally doubtful now is the notion that stability is achieved by the effective exclusion of many groups from involvement in the political processes, since resentment at such exclusion seems to be at least one important cause of the disruption itself. Given a demand for more democracy, there is considerable force in the traditional argument that the cure for the ills of democracy is more democracy.

Whether more democracy is a good in itself or is a good as a means to stability, its achievement presents many and difficult problems. In general, greater political equality is very closely bound up with movement towards equality in other areas, economic and educational. Where otherwise the search for more democracy will lead depends upon what is taken to be its justification. From one standpoint, the problem is to find ways in which governmental decisions might be more openly arrived at and more subject to public debate and evaluation. From another, the problem might be to discover the means by which presently disadvantaged wants or interests could be more adequately represented in the decision-making process. Or, if participation is the end in view, the search will be for ways in which small associations—voluntary organizations, the workplace, local government—might be further democratized and given greater weight within the whole political system. This is an agenda for analysis and empirical research as well as one for political action. It will no doubt be taken up only by those who see no contradiction between scholarship and the solution of social problems.

Index